THEATRES

D1646301

THE SHADOW FACTORY

by Howard Brenton

Th̶ .... ed at
Nuffield .... .uary 2018.

Foreword
Howard Brenton

This play is a love song to Southampton, written to celebrate a time of extreme danger and extreme human achievement in the town's history.

Sam Hodges, the artistic director of Nuffield Southampton Theatres, emailed me two years ago: was I interested in writing a play to open a brand-new theatre in the middle of the town?

Was I interested in breathing? I knew immediately I was going to say 'yes'. Back in 1976 I wrote the first new play to be performed in the National's Lyttleton Theatre. It was a great experience. In some mysterious way shows change a theatre: characters become ghosts in the walls, the carpets begin to change colour with feet shuffled during arguments about a play and spilt interval drinks. Architecture doesn't make a theatre, audiences and performances do. So, for both playwright and actors, there's nothing to match the excitement of being the first to have scenes seen and lines heard in a new theatre.

I met Sam in London's Old Vic coffee bar. We became very loud with enthusiasm! He told me of the bombing of the Woolston Spitfire factory by the German Luftwaffe in September 1940 and the shadow factories that replaced it.

I'd never heard the story. I was born in 1942, in my childhood I knew bomb sites – great places to play – but hardly anything of my parents' wartime experiences. They were a secretive generation: for example, it was only when my mother was eighty-three, and my father was dead, that she told me the family 'trekked' during the Blitz. Trekking was leaving your home to avoid the night bombing. Hundreds in British towns did it, in Liverpool, Glasgow, Portsmouth, Belfast: in Southampton people spent nights on the Common, even going as far as the New Forest. In the morning they would go back into the town to see if their homes still existed – just think, for a moment, of the traumatic experience of doing that.

So much is not said, or lies forgotten, even about a time like the Second World War. It was a shock to me while researching the play, and may be to audiences, to realise how powerful the Government was. Your house, your business could be requisitioned at a moment's notice under the Emergency Powers (Defence) Acts of 1939 and 1940. They made legal 'the taking of possession or control of any property or undertaking', requiring people 'to place themselves, their services and their property at the disposal of His Majesty'. Refuse and you would be imprisoned. From 1940 until 1945 Britain was effectively an authoritarian state run by Churchill's War Ministry in coalition with Atlee's Labour Party. Hitler's Government, fearing for their popularity, did not adopt measures similar to the Emergency Powers Acts until February 1943 when, in a notorious speech, Goebbels declared 'Total War'. Churchill and his ministers practised 'Total War' from the start, they trusted the people.

But there was consequence for our rulers. I write history plays because I'm fascinated by moments of crisis that cause great, even revolutionary change: for example my play *Anne Boleyn*, seen at Shakespeare's Globe, is about the English Reformation; two plays written for Hampstead Theatre, *55 Days* and *Drawing the Line*, are about Oliver Cromwell's decision to execute Charles II and Britain's withdrawal from India in 1947. Ugly times, brutal times but, in the end, they were for the good. I see 1940 as one of those moments and not for the obvious reason that we avoided defeat. People survived the Luftwaffe and knuckled down under the orders of the draconian War Ministry. Despair was far more widespread than is acknowledged but also a spirit of 'sod the lot of them' began to grow, undetected by the Government. In the end there would be payback. In 1945 Churchill got the shock of his life when the Labour Party won a general election with a majority of 145, then set about the most radical change in our country since the seventeenth century.

How true can history plays be? Well, they are yarns, not documentaries. But, though despite my best efforts there may be gaffes in the script, the aim was to try to be accurate about what happened in Southampton in the autumn of 1940. Then I invented a family, the Dimmocks, owners of a laundry and into just about everything in the town, to imagine what it would be like living through that time. Shakespeare did it! In *Part II* of *Henry IV* the fictitious Falstaff wanders around a battlefield in a real war, peopled with real historical characters.

And when the play's run is over, I hope Jackie Dimmock, her fictitious friend Polly, her mother and grandmother and her obstreperous, bloody-minded father Fred – along with my versions of the heroic Woolston Chief Engineer Len Gooch, the forceful Lord Beaverbrook and the brave, ill-treated Lady Cooper from Hursley House – are happy ghosts in Nuffield Southampton Theatres' new NST City.

A postscript. You've still got to eat, even if you are making history. There are exchanges about wartime diet in the play: Jackie Dimmock's grandmother makes an all but inedible carrot roll. The other day someone in the theatre asked if I had hosted a wartime dinner party, what would have been on my menu?

So here we go.

A rabbit stew – if I could shoot one, as Jackie does it the play. If not it would be a mock fish pie, made of boiled potatoes, boiled beans, a little lemon juice (much prized), two tablespoons of bloater paste, cayenne pepper and flour. Then a real treat: an upside-down apricot pudding, made with dried apricots which were difficult to get hold of. I'd probably have to have a word with Ma Dimmock about getting some 'on the quiet'.

Nuffield Southampton Theatres: One City, Two Venues

Nuffield Southampton Theatres (NST) is one of the UK's leading professional theatre companies, commissioning, developing and producing fresh, vital experiences through theatre.

NST has developed a profile and reputation for innovation and quality, delivering work on a national and international scale, taking work on tour around the UK, to London and Dubai, whilst acting as a major cultural force for good in the city of Southampton.

Howard Brenton's *The Shadow Factory* is the inaugural production at NST City, NST's second venue, in Southampton's city centre. NST City includes a flexible 450-seat main-house theatre, a 133-seat studio, screening facilities, rehearsal and workshop spaces.

NST will run the new city-centre venue alongside its existing theatre, NST Campus, on the University of Southampton's Highfield Campus. The produced programme is backed by a bespoke artist development programme, Laboratory, and extensive outreach and community projects, Connect.

Laboratory is the creative development programme for new work and new talent, through which NST collaborates with artists at all stages in their careers to experiment with new ideas.

Connect aims to enrich the experience for all, through a vibrant programme of engagement. Connect reaches over 17,000 people each year through a programme of creative activities, Youth Theatre, Drama Club, adult workshops and outreach projects, including RSC Open Stages.

NST is an Arts Council National Portfolio Organisation and a registered charity, receiving additional core funding from the University of Southampton and Southampton City Council.

In 2015, Nuffield Southampton Theatres was awarded Regional Theatre of the Year at The Stage Awards. In 2017, it won The Renee Stepham Award for Best Presentation of Touring Theatre for its brand new adaptation of Roald Dahl's *Fantastic Mr Fox*, in co-production with Curve Leicester and in association with Lyric Hammersmith, at the UK Theatre Awards.

CAST & TEAM

CAST

FRED/DOWDING	David Birrell
LIL/SYLVIA	Catherine Cusack
LADY COOPER/MA	Anita Dobson
JACKIE DIMMOCK	Lorna Fitzgerald
LORD BEAVERBROOK	Hilton McRae
POLLY	Shala Nyx
LEN GOOCH	Daniel York

Community Ensemble: Nicky Azor, Josie Bailey, Ollie Bruce, Daisy Collins, Chloe Coombes, Steve Cox, Sue Dashper, Caroline Dopica, Tetiana Dushenkivska, Jonathan Fulcher, Helen Gard, Dawn Gatrell, Julia Gavin, Clare Gott, Al Guthrie, Beatrice John, Hiva Hallaveh, Alan Matlock, Sam Momber, Jen Powell-Keilloh, Georgina Pugh, Grace Tarr, Adam Woods

CREATIVE TEAM

Writer	Howard Brenton
Director	Samuel Hodges

59 PRODUCTIONS

Design Director	Leo Warner
Set Designer	Jenny Melville
Video Designer	Akhila Krishnan
Lighting Designer	Matt Daw
Costume Designer	Molly Einchcomb
Producer	Ollie Hester
Assistant Video Designer	Hannah Fasching
Assistant Set Designer	Claudia Fragoso
Animators	Georgia Clegg, Emily Howells, Lawrence Watson
Design Team	Dale Croft, Gareth Damian Martin, Nicol Scott, Matthew Taylor
Video Programmer	Iain Syme
Video System Designer	Max Spielbichler
Design Intern	Felix Green

Sound Designers and Composers	Max and Ben Ringham
Musical Director	Candida Caldicot
Movement Director	Lucy Cullingford
Casting Director	Annelie Powell
Associate Director	Anthony Lau
Assistant Director	Gemma Aked-Priestley
Assistant Musical Director	Teddy Clements
Dialect Coach	Jacquie Crago

PRODUCTION TEAM

Production Manager	Andrew Quick
Assistant Production Manager	Andy Hunt
Company Stage Manager	Stuart Relph
Deputy Stage Manager	Karen Habens
Assistant Stage Manager	Christie Wilkes
Assistant Stage Manager	Jessica Rice
Stage Management Placement	Megan Naylor
Prop Maker	Jes Baines
Sound Operator	Rob Jones
Wardrobe Manager	Celia Grenville
Dresser	Olivia O'Grady
Costume Maker	Laila Jam
Make Up Artist	Flora Davies

Lighting Equipment	PRG & Evolve Technical Services
Automation	TAIT Stage Technologies
Sound Equipment	Stage Sound Services
Video Equipment	Stage Sound Services
Floral Spitfire	Claire Vidler – First Impression Flowers
With thanks to	National Theatre Props Hire, Glyndbourne Opera, Tangmere Military Aviation Museum, The Watermill, Weightwash Ltd

CAST

DAVID BIRRELL | FRED/DOWDING
Theatre includes: *The Threepenny Opera, Talking Heads, Educating Rita* (Bolton Octagon/Derby Theatre); *Wind in the Willows* (Original Cast UK tour); *Miss Atomic Bomb* (St. James Theatre); *The War Has Not Yet Started* (Theatre Royal Plymouth); *An Enemy of the People* – Best Supporting Actor Manchester Theatre Awards, *The Family Way, Journey's End* – Best Supporting Actor Manchester Theatre Awards (Bolton Octagon); *The Death of King Arthur* (Sam Wanamaker Playhouse); *Peter Pan, A Midsummer Night's Dream, Ragtime* (Regent's Park); *The Last Days of Troy* (Manchester Royal Exchange/Shakespeare's Globe); *Sweeney Todd* – Best Actor Nominee Manchester Theatre Awards, Best Performance in a Musical Nominee UK Theatre Awards (West Yorkshire Playhouse/Manchester Royal Exchange/Welsh National Opera); *A Little Night Music* (Guildford/West End); *Company* (Sheffield Crucible); *Passion, Grand Hotel* (Donmar); *Sweeney Todd* – Best Actor Scottish Critics Awards, Best Performance in a Musical Nominee UK Theatre Awards (Dundee Rep/National Theatre of Scotland); *The Secret Garden, Hapgood, Peter Pan* (Birmingham Rep/ West Yorkshire Playhouse); *The Real Thing* (Salisbury Playhouse); *Spamalot* (Original West End Cast); *Henry V* (Propeller); *Oh! What a Lovely War* (National Theatre); *The Gates of Paradise, The Jewess of Toledo, The Venetian Twins, Love's Labour's Lost, Moby Dick, The Tempest, Murder in the Cathedral, Hamlet, Columbus, Romeo and Juliet* (RSC).

Television and film includes: *Holy Flying Circus; Midsomer Murders; Buried; Angels.*

Recording credits include numerous plays and readings for BBC Radio and the original cast recording of Stiles and Drewe's *Peter Pan.*

CATHERINE CUSACK | LIL/SYLVIA
Theatre includes: *Judith: A Parting from the Body* (Arcola); *Fair Field* (Penned in the Margin/Shoreditch Town Hall); *Out of This World* (Macrobert Arts Centre/ tour); *Villette* (West Yorkshire Playhouse); *Dancing at Lughnasa, How Many Miles to Babylon?* and *The Crucible* (Lyric, Belfast); *The Seagull* (Headlong tour); *All That Fall* (Jermyn Street/New York); *Bingo* (Chichester Festival Theatre/revived Young Vic); *The Two Character Play* (Jermyn Street/Provincetown, USA); *The Early Bird, The Gigli Concert* (Finborough); *What Fatima Did* (Hampstead); *Fragile, Factory Girls* (Arcola); *Uncle Vanya* (Wilton's); Mary Stuart (National Theatre of Scotland); *The Venetian Twins* (Watermill); *Brontë, The Mill on the Floss* (Shared Experience); *Blood Red Saffron Yellow* (Drum, Plymouth); *Our Lady of Sligo* (NT/Out of Joint); *Measure for Measure* (English Touring Theatre); *Prayers of Sherkin* (Old Vic); *Mrs Warren's Profession* (Lyric Hammersmith); *Phaedra's Love* (Gate); *The Glass Menagerie* (Bolton).

Television includes: *The Last Days of Anne Boleyn; Doctors; Jonathan Creek; Ballykissangel; The Bill; Cadfael; Coronation Street; Doctor Who.*

Film includes: *Finding Neverland; Conspiracy of Silence; Boxed; The Lonely Passion of Judith Hearne.*

Radio: a regular on *Poetry Please* (BBC Radio 4); *The Raft of the Medusa; Hinterland; The Christmas Mysteries; The Girl at the Lion D'Or; Fragile; Cooking for Michael Collins.*

ANITA DOBSON | LADY COOPER/MA

Anita's many stage appearances include *Budgie* (Cambridge Theatre); Olga in *The Three Sisters* (Royal Court); Madame Jourdain in *Le Bourgeois Gentilhomme* (National Theatre); Donna in *Kvetch* (Garrick); Rose Weiss in *My Lovely Shayna Maidel* (Ambassadors); Kitty in *Charley's Aunt* (Aldwych); Gladys in *The Pyjama Game* (Victoria Palace); *The Vagina Monologues* (Arts Theatre/UK tour); Cleanthis in *The Island of Slaves* (Lyric Hammersmith); Nancy in *Frozen* (National Theatre) – nominated for an Olivier, Evening Standard and London Critics Award; Mama Morton in *Chicago* (Adelphi); Mrs Meers in *Thoroughly Modern Milly* (Shaftesbury); Gertrude in *Hamlet* (New Ambassadors/UK tour); Dolly Levi in *Hello Dolly* (Theatre Royal Lincoln/UK tour); Frau von Luber in Kurt Weill's opera *The Silver Lake* (Wexford Festival); Christ Harper in *Calendar Girls* (Noël Coward); Rika in *Two Sisters* (Eastbourne and Brighton); Carabosse in *Sleeping Beauty* (Richmond); *Strictly Come Dancing Live!*; Joan Crawford in *Bette and Joan* (Arts Theatre); Mistress Quickly in *Merry Wives of Windsor* (RSC); Jacosta in Steven Berkoff's production of *Oedipus* (Edinburgh Festival at the Pleasance Grand); Parfait in *Carnival Of The Animals*; Miss Austin in *Crush – A Girl's Own Musical*; Stella in the all-star concert version of *Follies* (Royal Albert Hall); Mrs Hardcastle in *She Stoops To Conquer* (Theatre Royal, Bath) and most recently as Madame Morrible in *Wicked* (Apollo Victoria).

As Angie Watts in *EastEnders*, Anita Dobson was one of the most popular characters on television, winning her the Pye Award for Television Personality of the Year, the Daily Mirror's Actress of the Year and the TV Times Actress of the Year award, voted by the readers.

Other television includes: *Leave Him To Heaven; Nanny; The House of Lurking Death; Up the Elephant and Round the Castle; Split Ends; The World of Eddie Weary; Red Dwarf; Rab C Nesbitt; Smokescreen; I'll Be Watching You; Dangerfield; The Famous Five; Highlander; Get Well Soon; Junk; Sunburn; The Stretch; Hearts and Bones; Urban Gothic; NCS Manhunt; Fun at the Funeral Parlour; The Last Detective; Doctors; New Tricks; The Bill; Hotel Babylon; Casualty; Katy Brand's Big Ass Show; 12 O'clock Girls; Green Santa; Little Crackers 'My First Nativity'; Coming Up (Hooked); Sadie J; Moving On; Pompidou; Holby City; Armada; Call the Midwife; The Worst Witch;* two series of *The Rebel.*

Film includes: *Seaview Knights; Beyond Bedlam; The Tichborne Claimant; The Revengers' Comedies; Darkness Falls; Charlie; Soltary; The Rise of the Krays; The Fall of The Krays; London Road* (taken from the acclaimed National Theatre production directed by Rufus Norris) and *The Fight.*

LORNA FITZGERALD | JACKIE DIMMOCK

Lorna was born in London and has appeared in various television roles since the age of six including *Casualty, The World According to Bex, Cherished & The Golden Hour.* She has most recently played the role of Abi Branning in *EastEnders* since 2006 and made her final screen appearance as Abi in January 2018.

The Shadow Factory marks her stage debut.

HILTON MCRAE | LORD BEAVERBROOK

Theatre includes: in the West End: *Les Liaisons Dangereuses* (West End/Broadway); *1984*; *End of the Rainbow* (Best Supporting Actor Nominee Olivier Awards); *Rabbit*; *My One and Only*; *Mamma Mia*; *Les Misérables*; *Miss Saigon*; *Piaf.*

Other theatre includes: *Uncle Vanya* (Almeida); *The Cocktail Party* (Print Room); *The Kreutzer Sonata* (The Gate/La MaMa, New York); *Timon of Athens, Caroline, or Change* (National Theatre); *The Danton Affair, Troilus and Cressida, As You Like It, Total Eclipse, Much Ado About Nothing, The Innocent, Anthony and Cleopatra, Captain Swing, The Churchill Play, The Merchant of Venice, Factory Birds, Bandits* (RSC); *Experimentum Mundi* (Edinburgh International Festival); *The Oresteia Trilogy* (Fisher Centre, New York); *Rock 'n' Roll* (Manchester Library); *The Wizard of Oz* (Royal Festival Hall); *Weapons of Happiness* (Finborough); *Hamlet* (Royal Theatre Northampton); *The Tempest* (Southwark Playhouse); *Peer Gynt* (Arcola); *The Front Page* (Donmar); *Othello, A Doll's House* (Birmingham Rep); *Hedda Gabler* (Manchester Royal Exchange); *Macbeth* (Dundee Rep); *LayOff/Yobbo Nowt* (7:84).

Film includes: *Darkest Hour; Denial; The Sense of an Ending; Macbeth; Far from the Madding Crowd; Mansfield Park; Return of the Jedi; Secret Rapture; Greystoke; The French Lieutenant's Woman.*

Television includes: *Endeavour; Injustice; Zen, Red Riding Trilogy – 1983; The Execution of Gary Glitter; Lewis; Frances Tuesday; Murder City; Baby Father; Serious & Organised; Deacon Brodie; King of Hearts; First Take; To Each His Own; Roll Over Beethoven; Poppyland; Forever Young.*

SHALA NYX | POLLY

Theatre includes: Rayah in *Cookies* (Theatre Royal Haymarket); 1 in *Every You Every Me* (Oxford Playhouse/Reading Rep); *Her* (Brolly Productions); Moo Moo & Wify in *Bollywood Jack* (Tara Arts); Pheobe in *As You Like It*, Benvolio in *Romeo and Juliet* (GB Theatre); Somerset/Clarence in *HENRY VI* (Wales Millennium Centre); Katie in *Dogtag* (Theatre West); Older Sister in *Stoning Mary* (The Lonon Criterion); Miss Prue in *Love for Love* (Bristol Old Vic); Brigida in *The Heresy of Love*, (Bristol Old Vic Studio); Sister in *Random*; Claire/Lane in *Road* (Circomedia); Heidi in *Sauce for the Goose* (West Country tour); Courtesan in *The Comedy of Errors* (Assembly George Square Studios); Freya in *Ragnarok* (BOVTS Studio); Daw in *The Nativity* (The Redgrave); Saint Monica in *Last Days of Judas Iscatriot* (BOVTS Studio); Sarah in *Speaking in Tongues* (BOVTS Studio); Mustardseed in *A Midsummer Night's Dream*; Perfectionist in *4.48 Psychosis*, Sophie Fevvers in *Nights at the Circus*, Nurse in *The Love of a Nightingale*, Crookfinger Jake in *The Threepenny Opera* (Fourth Monkey Theatre Company); Hayley in *We, The Undersigned, Imaginary Forces* (Southwark Playhouse); Rosario in *The Search For Love* (The Bridge).

Film credits include: Rachel in *Knock Down Ginger* – BFI London Film Festival 2016 Official Selection, *A Safe Space*; *Bare All.*

Television includes: Meena Mander in *Bottom Knocker Street* (ITV).

Short film includes: *Unlike* (Channel 4); *Electro Girl*; *Candle To Water.*

Radio includes: *Carleton Hobbs* (BBC); *Upside Down and Back to Front*; *The Incident.*

DANIEL YORK | LEN GOOCH

Theatre includes: *The Merchant of Venice, The Country Wife, Moby Dick, Snow in Midsummer, Dido Queen of Carthage* (RSC); *Welcome Home, Captain Fox!* (Donmar Warehouse); *The World of Extreme Happiness* (National Theatre); *Our American Cousin, We Know Where You Live, P'yongyang* (Finborough); *Une Tempete* (Gate); *Porcelain* (Royal Court); *The Magic Fundoshi* (Lyric Studio, Hammersmith); *Hamlet* (Riverside Studios); *Sun is Shining* (King's Head/Battersea Arts Centre/Off-Broadway, New York); *The Changeling* (Southwark Playhouse); *Branded* (Old Vic); *Turandot* (Hampstead); *The Tempest* (NT 'Shakespeare Unplugged' tour); *Measure for Measure* (Manchester Library); *Nativity* (Birmingham Rep); *King Lear* (Shangahi/UK tour); *The Good Woman of Setzuan* (Leicester Haymarket); *In the Bag* (Traverse, Edinburgh); *Tartuffe, Romeo and Juliet* (Basingstoke Haymarket); *Five Tanks* (Hackney Empire); *Made In England* (Manchester Contact/Birmingham Rep); *Blind* (Courtyard); *The Birds* (Aquila US tour).

Singapore: *The Glass Menagerie; Kiss of the Spider Woman; The Importance of Being Earnest* (also Macau and Brisbane); *Freud's Last Session; Dealer's Choice; Boeing Boeing; Starring Hitler as Jekyll and Hyde.*

Television includes: *Whitechapel; Moving On; Waking the Dead; Casualty; Peggy Su!; Chambers; The Bill; Supper at Emmaus; A Fish Named Tao; Hollyoaks.*

Film includes: *Scarborough; The Receptionist; Rogue Trader; The Beach; Faraway; Act of Grace; Doom.*

Radio includes: *Doggie's Nirvana* (BBC Radio Three); *Romeo and Juliet, The Monkey King, Dead Lines* (BBC World Service); *Say It With Flowers, Inspector Chen* (two series), *The Odyssey.*

Projects include: *Telemachus, Death at the Airport* (BBC Radio Four).

CREATIVE TEAM

HOWARD BRENTON | WRITER

Howard Brenton has written over 50 plays. His most recent credits include *Paul* (National Theatre), *In Extremis,* later retitled *Eternal Love* (Shakespeare's Globe and tour), *Never So Good* (National Theatre), *Anne Boleyn* (Shakespeare's Globe, plus revival and tour, winner of the Whatsonstage Best Play Award and UK Theatre Awards Best Touring Production), *55 Days* (Hampstead), *#aiww: The Arrest of Ai Weiwei* (Hampstead), *The Guffin* (one-act play, NT Connections), *Drawing the Line* (Hampstead), *Doctor Scroggy's War* (Shakespeare's Globe), *Ransomed* (one-act play, Salisbury Playhouse), *Lawrence After Arabia* (Hampstead) and *The Blinding Light* (Jermyn Street). Versions of classics include *The Life of Galileo* and *Danton's Death* (National Theatre) and *Goethe's Faust* (RSC). Other adaptations include *The Ragged Trousered Philanthropists* (Liverpool Everyman and Chichester Festival Theatre), *Dances of Death* (Gate) and *Miss Julie* (Theatre by the Lake, Keswick and Jermyn Street Theatre). For television, he wrote thirteen episodes of the first four series of the BBC Television Drama *Spooks* – Best Television Drama Series BAFTA 2003.

SAMUEL HODGES | DIRECTOR

Samuel Hodges is Director and CEO of Nuffield Southampton Theatres. His productions for NST include *Dedication – Shakespeare and Southampton*, following *The Glass Menagerie* in 2015. Previously he founded the HighTide Festival Theatre in 2007 and was the Artistic Director for five years, during which time he produced over 25 new plays, co-producing with the National Theatre, The Old Vic and the Bush Theatre, amongst others. Between 2012 and 2014, he ran the Criterion Theatre in London's West End, for whom he curated a late-night programme and a one-off summer season of new work to celebrate the London Olympics.

59 PRODUCTIONS | DESIGNER

59 Productions is the multi award-winning company of artists behind the video design of the Opening Ceremony of the London 2012 Olympic Games and *War Horse*, the design and creative direction of the record-breaking *David Bowie is* exhibition, and video design of Christopher Wheeldon's celebrated stage adaptation of *An American in Paris* – Tony Award 2015. Led by directors **Leo Warner**, **Mark Grimmer**, **Lysander Ashton** and **Richard Slaney**, 59 Productions are world-leading specialists in design for stage and live events. They are the go-to team for generating creative and technical ideas to realise ambitious artistic projects across a range of disciplines: from architectural projection mapping to exhibition design, VR experiences to events, theatrical design to technical consultancy. In 2017, 59 Productions began producing its own theatrical work, opening its first full-scale production, Paul Auster's *City of Glass* (HOME, Manchester, Lyric, Hammersmith). Current and upcoming projects also include, *Oslo* (Lincoln Center & National Theatre), *The (R)evolution of Steve Jobs* (Santa Fe Opera), *Marnie* (The Met Opera & ENO), *Reflections* (a four-day projection-mapping event to mark the twentieth anniversary of the Guggenheim Museum Bilbao) and *A Perfect Harmony* (specially commissioned as the centrepiece of the weekend-long celebrations for the re-opening of Washington's Freer|Sackler museums in October 2017).

BEN AND MAX RINGHAM | SOUND DESIGNERS AND COMPOSERS

Awards include: OffWestEnd Awards Best Sound Designer Winner 2014 (*Ring*, BAC), IMGA Excellence in Sound Design Award Winner 2014 (*Papa Sangre II*), Best Sound Design Laurence Olivier Award Nomination 2012 (*The Ladykillers*), Best Sound Design Laurence Olivier Award Nomination 2009 (*Piaf*), Best Overall Achievement in an Affiliate Theatre Laurence Olivier Award Winner (as part of the creative team) 2009 (*The Pride*).

Theatre includes: *Parliament Square, Our Town* (Manchester Royal Exchange); *Apologia* (Trafalgar Studios); *King Lear* (Chichester Festival Theatre); *Twilight Song* (Park); *Gloria* (Hampstead); *The Importance of Being Earnest* (Theatr Clwyd); *Gaslight* (ATG); *Pygmalion* (Headlong/West Yorkshire Playhouse/Nuffield Southampton Theatres); *The Miser* (Garrick); *The Pitchfork Disney* (Shoreditch Town Hall); *Lunch & The Bow of Ulysses* (Trafalgar Studios);*The Dresser* (Duke of York's); *After Miss Julie* (Theatre Royal Bath); *The Mighty Walzer* (Manchester Royal Exchange); *Doctor Faustus, The Maids* (Trafalgar Studios); *Deathtrap* (Salisbury Playhouse); *The Government Inspector* (Birmingham Rep); *Raz* (Assembly/Riverside Studios); *Queen Anne* (RSC/Theatre Royal Haymarket); *Ben Hur, A Wolf in Snakeskin Shoes* (Tricycle); *La Musica* (Young Vic); *The Mentalists* (Wyndham's); *Raz* (Assembly, Edinburgh); *We Want You to Watch* (National Theatre Temporary Space); *Ah, Wilderness!* (Young Vic); *Multitudes* (Tricycle); *The Ruling Class* (Trafalgar Transformed); *The Walworth Farce* (Olympia, Dublin); *2071* (Royal Court); *Minetti* (EIF); *Richard III* (Traf Transformed); *Adler and Gibb* (Royal Court); *Dawn French* (UK tour); *Fiction* (UK tour); *Blithe Spirit* (Gielgud/US tour); *Boeing Boeing* (Sheffield Crucible); *I Can't Sing* (London Palladium); *The Full Monty* (Sheffield/Noël Coward); *Jeeves and Wooster* (Duke of York's); and *Ben Hur* (Watermill).

Ben and Max are associate artists with the Shunt collective and two-thirds of the band Superthriller. In 2013 they designed 'Papa Sangre II' a sound-based IOS game for digital arts company Somethin' Else. They are also co-creators of the immersive theatre company Wiretapper.

CANDIDA CALDICOT | MUSICAL DIRECTOR

Upcoming credits include: *Snow White* (Lighthouse Theatre).

Musical Director credits include: *Queen Anne* (Theatre Royal Haymarket); *Woyzeck* (Old Vic); *Peter Pan* (Regent's Park); *Beauty and the Beast* (Lighthouse Theatre); *Beyond the Fence* (Sky Arts, Arts Theatre); *It's a Mad World My Masters* (English Touring Theatre); *Hecuba, The Witch of Edmonton, The Heresy of Love, The Heart of Robin Hood* (RSC); *The Tempest* (RSC, US Suitcase tour); *Love's Labour's Lost* (Oxford Shakespeare Company); *Galileo* (Birmingham Rep); *A Soldier In Every Son* (international tour); *The Vaudevillians* (Lowry Theatre/Charing Cross).

As Composer: *Zeraffa Giraffa* (Little Angel/Omnibus); *Buckets* (Orange Tree); *4 Pepys* (Wilderness Festival); multiple summer seasons with Iris Theatre; *Macbeth* (Shakespeare in Styria); *Once Upon a Time* (Booktrust tour); *The Hostage* (Southwark Playhouse).

Candida was Musical Director on two new musicals for NYMT: *Prodigy* (& Orchestrator, St James Theatre); and *The Battle of the Boat* (Rose, Kingston). An original cast album for *Prodigy* has been released.

Candida trained at Cambridge University where she received a University Instrumental Award for piano. She also plays the oboe, violin and accordion.

LUCY CULLINGFORD | MOVEMENT DIRECTOR

Lucy collaborates regularly with the RSC and recent productions in the role of Movement Director include: *Coriolanus, Snow in Midsummer*, Greg Doran's groundbreaking production of *The Tempest, Don Quixote* and *The Jew of Malta*.

Other high-profile credits include: *King Lear*, with Ian Mckellen (Chichester Festival Theatre) and *Constellations* (Royal Court, West End, Broadway and national tour).

Lucy was the RSC/Warwick University Creative Fellow in Residence where she directed *The Renaissance Body*. The piece was staged to mark the reopening of the Swan Theatre, Stratford and as a live installation at the British Museum as part of the Shakespeare: Staging The World Exhibition for the World Shakespeare Festival in 2012.

Further movement credits include: *East is East* (Northern Stage); *Jenufa* (revival, Grange Park Opera); *Abigail's Party* and *Talking Heads* (Theatre Royal Bath); *The 101 Dalmations* and *Of Mice and Men* (Birmingham Rep); *The BFG* (Bolton Octagon); *The Night Before Christmas* (West Yorkshire Playhouse); *Flare Path* (The Original Theatre Co); *The Mother, Intimate Apparel* and *The Double* (Ustinov, Bath); *The Spanish Golden Age Season* (Ustinov/Arcola/Belgrade).

Recent choreography credits include: *The Last Mermaid* with Charlotte Church (Wales Millenium Centre); *Alice In Wonderland* (CBBC); *The Secret Adversary* (Watermill); *Rusalka* (revival Royal Danish Opera). Lucy has worked as Children's Dance Repetiteur on *Matilda The Musical* (RSC) in Stratford-upon-Avon and the West End.

Lucy has an MA in Movement Studies from The Royal Central School of Speech and Drama.

ANNELIE POWELL | CASTING DIRECTOR CDG

Annelie is Head of Casting at Nuffield Southampton Theatres and a freelance Casting Director. She was formerly Assistant Casting Director at the Royal Shakespeare Company, where she cast main house productions, alongside many readings and development workshops over the five years she was there.

Recent credits include: *Hamlet, King Lear, Imperium* (RSC); *Freedom on the Tyne; Fantastic Mr Fox* (Nuffield Southampton Theatres), amongst others.

ANTHONY LAU | ASSOCIATE DIRECTOR

Anthony is currently Resident Director on *Ink* in the West End.

He was Laboratory Associate Director at Nuffield Southampton Theatres in 2015, supported by the BBC Performing Arts Fund, and trained as a director at LAMDA.

Credits as Director include: *A Better Man* and *The Cherry Orchard* Parallel (Young Vic); *Juicy and Delicious* (Nuffield Southampton Theatres); *The Common Land* (Rose, Kingston); *Dreaming in America* (world premiere, Shoreditch Town Hall); *Still Life/Red Peppers* (Old Red Lion); *The Taste of Us* (HighTide Festival); *I Am A Camera* (Southwark Playhouse); *Tape* (CounterCulture, London Bridge) and *Orphans* (Linbury Studio LAMDA).

Credits as Assistant Director include: *First Light* (Chichester Festival Theatre); *The Glass Menagerie* (Nuffield Southampton Theatres); *The Hudsucker Proxy* (Liverpool Playhouse/Nuffield Southampton Theatres); *King Lear* (Chichester Festival Theatre /BAM, New York); *Mint* (Royal Court); *Canvas* (Chichester Festival theatre); *Bingo* (Young Vic); *Hungry Ghosts* (Orange Tree) and *An Inspector Calls* (Paris tour).

GEMMA AKED-PRIESTLEY | ASSISTANT DIRECTOR
Leverhulme Arts Scholar and recipient of the JMK Regional Assistant Director Bursary.

Gemma is the assistant director for The Mono Box and the founder of PLAYSTART. Her passion is new writing that engages hearts, grows imaginations and challenges what we think we know to be true.

Directing credits include: *The Narcissist* (Flux/The Hen and Chickens); *Passing* (The Bunker/ Women@RADA); *Grimm: An Untold Tale* (Underbelly, Edinburgh Fringe); *Tender Napalm* (Karamel Club Theatre).

Assistant directing credits include: *Thebes Land* (Arcola); *Tonight With Donny Stixx* (The Bunker); *Lockhart* (The Bernie Grant Arts Centre).

Gemma trained at Mountview Academy of Theatre Arts on the MA Theatre Directing course and at the University of East Anglia.

THE JMK TRUST
The JMK Trust was founded in 1997 in memory of a theatre director of thrilling promise, James Menzies-Kitchin, who died suddenly and unexpectedly at the age of 28. The Trust runs the annual JMK Young Director's Award and works with theatres around the UK through its regional programme to discover and support emerging theatre directors. Its assistant director bursary, funded by The Leverhulme Trust Arts Scholarships Award, is another part of its work which enables directors to learn new skills through practical experience. For more details about the JMK Trust and their work please visit **www.jmktrust.org.**

TEDDY CLEMENTS | ASSISTANT MUSIC DIRECTOR
Teddy studied music at the University of Southampton and is a musical director, composer, arranger, vocal coach and audition pianist.

Musical Director Credits include: *Obella* (Guildford School of Acting, University of Portsmouth, University of Winchester); *Fortune Lane* (Union); *Things We're Learning Now* (Battersea Barge); *Tomorrow, Maybe* (Actor's Centre, Bridge House Theatre, C Nova, Omnibus); *Blueprints* (Theatre Royal Winchester); *ICONIC* (Century Club, Stage Door); *Kerry Ellis & Velma Celli* (The Stage Door); *Theory of Relativity* (Theatre Royal Winchester); *A Christmas Carol* (Luton Library Theatre).

Composer Credits, as part of 'Amies & Clements': *Obella* (Guildford School of Acting, University of Portsmouth, University of Winchester); *Tomorrow, Maybe* (Actor's Centre, Bridge House Theatre, C Nova, Omnibus); *Blueprints* (Theatre Royal Winchester).

JACQUIE CRAGO | DIALECT COACH
Jacqui is a freelance voice, text and dialect coach in regional theatres, the Royal Shakespeare Company and the Royal National Theatre. She is a regular coach on *War Horse*. She also leads workshops and projects for drama schools and opera courses. Jacquie works as an actor and director when time and opportunity allow.

THE SHADOW FACTORY

Howard Brenton

In memory of Michael Bogdanov

Characters

TOWN   BIG HOUSE

JACQUELINE
    'JACKIE' DIMMOCK

POLLY STRIDE
    Jackie's friend

LILIAN 'LIL' DIMMOCK   & SYLVIA MEINSTER
    Jackie's mother   *a member of Lady*
                                    Cooper's staff

ALFRED 'FRED'   & AIR CHIEF MARSHAL
    DIMMOCK   SIR HUGH DOWDING
    Jackie's father

MARY 'MA' DIMMOCK   & LADY COOPER
    Fred's mother

BACK AND FORTH BETWEEN TOWN AND BIG HOUSE

LORD 'MAX' BEAVERBROOK

LEN GOOCH

There is a COMMUNITY CHORUS.

The action takes place in Southampton, the grounds and rooms of Hursley House, just outside the town, and in the Ministry for Aircraft Production, London.

Time: autumn of 1940.

This text went to press before the end of rehearsals and so may differ slightly from the play as performed.

ACT ONE

Scene One

JACKIE DIMMOCK (*twenty-one years*) *and her friend* POLLY STRIDE (*twenty-four years*). JACKIE *has an air rifle,* POLLY *has a basket.*

JACKIE (*aside*). A lovely day. September, 1940. You just want to reach out and – eat it!

POLLY (*aside*). Sneaked up here after work. Her idea.

JACKIE (*aside*). Grounds of Lady Cooper's stately home. Hursley House.

POLLY (*aside*). Dark green, yellowy.

JACKIE (*aside*). Woods and fields. And money.

POLLY (*aside*). Really pretty.

JACKIE. There's one!

She fires the rifle. Misses.

Oh sod it!

POLLY. Do you think we really ought to do this?

JACKIE. Come off it, Poll, they say the old girl's got a Mercedes Benz, a Panhard Dynamic and three Rolls-Royces. She's loaded! I don't think she counts her rabbits.

POLLY. Jackie, it's poaching.

JACKIE. Great, in't it. Course, if I had a real gun, not this pea-shooting air thing, I could bag one of Lady Da-di-da's deers.

POLLY. I think you say 'deer', not deers.

JACKIE. Ooh, pisscake, Polly the Precise!

POLLY. Deer is a collective noun, that's all.

JACKIE. Yeah yeah, Miss Clever Clogs.

POLLY. Let's have our picnic.

JACKIE. And our beer.

They sit. POLLY *takes out a rug from the basket and they lay it down. They sit on the rug.* POLLY *takes two bottles of beer out of the basket and a bottle opener. She opens the bottles of beer, hands one to* JACKIE. *They chink bottles and drink. They relax.*

POLLY *takes out a sketchpad.*

Think they'll come today?

POLLY. If not it'll be tomorrow.

A pause. JACKIE *drinking beer,* POLLY *drawing.*

JACKIE. I know a man who's got a Lee-Enfield.

POLLY. An army gun? Who?

JACKIE. That'd kill a deer. Blow its head right off!

POLLY. But if you did, really did, shoot a deer, what would you do with it?

JACKIE. Eddy Rose the butcher would hang it for us and we'd sell it on the – (*Touches her nose.*) Eddy's a friend of my dad's. You know – trouser legs.

POLLY. Trouser what?

JACKIE (*low, quick*). Masons.

POLLY. Your family and its fiddles –

JACKIE. It's the war! You find yourself doing things you never – I mean, look at you. Only woman in the Woolston factory office and twenty-four years old, designing Spitfires?

POLLY. I'm not designing them!

JACKIE. What you doing then?

POLLY. You know I can't say.

JACKIE. Is it the wings? I imagine you doing the wings.

POLLY. Stop it, you know it's secret.

JACKIE. Secret, secret, I dunno why they don't keep the whole war secret. Not let people know why they're getting bombed at all. Bang! Oh, who bombed my house? Was it Germans in a Junkers 88? Not allowed to say, it's a secret.

POLLY. Jackie, sometimes you are very silly.

JACKIE. Yeah, in't I.

JACKIE *drinks. She is restless,* POLLY *is content, drawing.*

POLLY. Anyway, who is this man with an army gun?

JACKIE. Oh he's nothing much.

POLLY. But he's in the army.

JACKIE. Actually he's with the machine-gun post on the roof at Woolston.

POLLY. Not – Not Billy Lewis.

JACKIE (*a shrug*). Maybe.

POLLY. You're going out with Billy Lewis!

JACKIE. Oh, we're well past 'going out'.

POLLY. I see. I hope you know what you're doing.

JACKIE. Course I do. (*A beat.*) Can I tell you a secret?

POLLY. Must you?

JACKIE. I'm going to marry him.

POLLY *is stunned.*

POLLY. But he's –

JACKIE. Yes I give in, yes he is gorgeous.

POLLY. He is gorgeous, very. But I mean, Jackie – he's from Portsmouth.

JACKIE. So?

POLLY. So what does your dad say about you marrying a Pompeyite?

JACKIE. I haven't told him yet.

POLLY. Rather you than me.

JACKIE. Rabbits!

JACKIE springs up with the air gun and fires.

Did I get one?

POLLY. Don't know, I –

JACKIE. Did, I did, I got one!

She runs off as –

LADY COOPER (*seventy-one years*) *and* SYLVIA
MEINSTER (*fifty-two years*) *enter.* LADY COOPER *has
American in her voice, tempered by years in England.*
SYLVIA *speaks English cut-glass.*

SYLVIA. That young woman's got a gun!

LADY COOPER. Yes, interesting.

SYLVIA. If she is poaching I will telephone the police.

LADY COOPER. She's having a bit of fun.

SYLVIA. With a firearm?

LADY COOPER. Air rifle.

SYLVIA. It's disgraceful, floozies from the town, disporting
themselves in the grounds. Leaving rubbish in the bushes,
men.

LADY COOPER. They leave men in the bushes? Well! Hang
'em up on the fences, as we do with stoats and the like. Scare
off all this male wildlife.

SYLVIA. I'm speaking figuratively.

LADY COOPER. Sylvia, I know you care so much for me, the
house, the estate. But I don't mind people picnicking. It must
be horrible down in the town.

SYLVIA. But one does hear of – excesses, bad behaviour.

LADY COOPER. They are getting bombed.

SYLVIA. That is no excuse for displays of drink and wantoness.

LADY COOPER. Sylvia, what a stickler you are.

SYLVIA. War is a great opportunity for self-discipline.

LADY COOPER. And a party now and then.

Enter JACKIE, *gun in one hand, a dead rabbit held up in the other.*

JACKIE. Supper!

SYLVIA. They *are* poaching!

LADY COOPER (*she calls out*). Young lady, I do believe that is my rabbit.

For a moment the two groups stare at each other.

POLLY. That's her, Lady Cooper.

JACKIE. Now we're for it, oh well.

SYLVIA. I will ring the police.

LADY COOPER. I think the Southampton Constabulary have other things to deal with, don't you?

JACKIE grabs up the rug and basket, both arms full, with gun and rabbit.

JACKIE. Run for it.

POLLY. No!

Suddenly there is the roar of a Spitfire, flying very low and in trouble.

Both couples duck.

JACKIE drops the basket and blanket. Beer bottles roll out.

JACKIE. Spitfire!

POLLY. A Mk V –

SYLVIA. He'll crash into the house!

LADY COOPER. God help us!

POLLY. There must be an air fight, out over the Channel.

POLLY runs towards LADY COOPER *and* SYLVIA *then stops.*

Don't worry! He's making for Eastleigh!

LADY COOPER. But he's on fire –

POLLY. His fuel pipe's hit. But he'll make it.

LADY COOPER. How do you know that?

POLLY. Because he will.

> LADY COOPER *and* SYLVIA *stare at* POLLY. *She looks up at the sky.*

> The thing is, what's he been fighting out there?

JACKIE. Sorry about your rabbit. I'll –

> *She is about to lay it on the ground.*

LADY COOPER. No, dear, it's yours.

JACKIE. Oh. Thanks very much.

SYLVIA. Really, your ladyship, I –

LADY COOPER. But make sure, if you come up here again, you don't leave bottles in the grass. The deer have tender feet.

> POLLY, *a hint of an awkward curtsy.*

> *The sound of many aircraft begins.*

POLLY. Thank you very much, your ladyship.

JACKIE. Yes, thanks, I'm sure.

> JACKIE *nudges* POLLY. *They back away, then are running.*

SYLVIA. Mary, you are just too nice.

LADY COOPER. Don't you think it's worth trying to be, these terrible days?

> SYLVIA *is irritated but before she can reply the sound of approaching aircraft is now loud. They look up at the sky.*

> POLLY *and* JACKIE, *nearly off the stage, stop and look up.*

> *The sound of bombing.*

POLLY. They have come.

JACKIE. Is it Woolston?

SYLVIA. We must go to the cellars –

> *But* LADY COOPER *is transfixed, staring out.*

POLLY. Junkers 88s. A whole wing.

JACKIE. Say it's not Woolston!

LADY COOPER. The black planes, the clouds, it all whirls above you, it's almost beautiful. You go dizzy.

SYLVIA. Mary!

LADY COOPER. It's not the house they want to bomb, it's Southampton. The poor people down there –

SYLVIA. We are going in the cellar!

She is dragging LADY COOPER *away.*

JACKIE. Billy's on duty. On the roof.

They turn to run.

Blackout.

Scene Two

Chorus of Townspeople

CHORUS.
 Air-raid drill
  Blitz drill
   But is this one real?

 False alarm or real? You never know.

 You get all the way down to the shelter
  Nothing happens
 Sit there, nothing happens

 And are the wardens keeping an eye
 Out for looters
 Just cos this is a war
 Human nature doesn't change

 No! Human nature doesn't change

Suddenly they react as if a shockwave has hit them.
Looking up, mouths open.

That was real!
                    Over by the river
                              Woolston way
Archery Road

Three families introduce themselves.

Austin House Garage
     Family garage, Barker family built it up
                    Corner of Bannister Road and The Avenue
We Barkers have got our Blitz drill down to a T

The Hollys of Holly Brook Ironmonger's, we live above
     the shop
                    But out in the garden
                                        Family pride and joy
Anderson Shelter! (Dad put in bunks and all...)

Botley's Store convenience food
                    Botley's forever and for everything
                              Cauliflowers to colic med'cine and
     brown paper
Public shelter on the corner, quick get down there

Barkers have been Southampton since when!
                    Hollys – Southampton, way back!
                              Botleys Southampton born and bred!

Quick, this one's for real
Bolt the shutters
Fill up the bath
Fill up the sinks
Water if there's fire
Suitcases of your stuff
Keep the cases ready in the hall
Take 'em to the shelter
Change of clothes candles soap
Photo album of the family

Cos if

Cos if

Come the all-clear
And you come out the shelter
And your house has gone

Gone

You'll have a change of clothes
    And photos to remember

The three families.

Barkers stay put in the raids
                Our house is our shelter
                    Gas turned off
Bath sinks filled up, windows opened cos of flying glass

Plenty of candles
            And under we get!
Under the big mahogany table in the front room
                Barkers stay put!

Hollys to their Anderson
            Dad's pride and joy
                All kindsa mod-cons
The Government says no paraffin lamps

    But Dad's made a safety hood outta Tate 'n' Lyle tins

Botleys do the drill extra-fast
            Shelter on the corner
                Lock up the shop quick

Get to the shelter first
    Only room in there for twelve
Keep calm and carry on
    Calm
Calm
    Calm

*Hunched, listening. They react as if hearing a huge
explosion.*

This is a heavy one
A heavy one
Woolston way

It's Supermarine
They're going for Supermarine
They're flattening the factory
It's Supermarine

Scene Three

The bombed Woolston factory. A barrier. Much activity,
POLICEMEN *and* FIREMEN.

Ener POLLY *and* JACKIE.

Shock.

Freeze the scene.

JACKIE (*aside*). The – look of it – dust in the air – Snakes, no
not snakes, fire hoses, all higgledy-piggledy, everywhere
sopping wet – and – grey – shapes of things that are all
wrong, tumbled down kiddies' bricks – sticking-up girders,
twisted. And the stink! Like tar from one of them nightmare
machines that do the roads but in your nose, burnt. And you
see but don't see, lying in bricks half a person, no legs.

They stand still, looking.

JACKIE *turns away sharply and clings to* POLLY. POLLY
continues to stare.

POLLY (*aside*). Could I draw that? What a terrible thing to think.

Animate the scene.

Oh God, the drawing office –

JACKIE. Polly, the roof – it's gone.

POLLY. We don't know anything. Look, I've got a pass. I'll go
and find out about Billy –

JACKIE. Bless you, Poll!

LEN GOOCH *enters.* POLLY *sees him.*

POLLY. Mr Gooch! Mr Gooch!

JACKIE. Oh yes, Mr Gooch!

He comes over to them.

LEN. Miss Stride, you shouldn't be here. It's not safe.

POLLY. But the drawing office –

LEN. They're saving what they can.

POLLY. I've got to help.

LEN. I told you, it's not safe, there are incendiaries that haven't gone off.

JACKIE. She works here much as you.

LEN. And I do not know what you are doing here, Jackie Dimmock.

JACKIE. That's my business.

POLLY. The drawings for the new machine-gun cowling. I want to make sure they're safe.

He hesitates, then.

LEN. All right, but go with a policeman and do everything the firemen say.

JACKIE (*to* POLLY). Find him.

POLLY. I will.

POLLY *hurries away with a* POLICEMAN *and exits.*

LEN. Jackie, the power's out and the phones all over town, your mum and dad will be worried sick.

JACKIE. What happened to the men on the roof?

He stares at her.

The machine-gun post, on the roof, the men?

LEN. The whole roof's gone. And the army post.

They stare at each other.

Go home. Looks like some of the raiders dumped their bombs the other side of the river. Go and make sure your family's safe.

And now she is staring off.

You've got to grow up, Jackie, take responsibility.

JACKIE. It's Billy! He's all right. Billy!

She runs into the cordon.

LEN. For Godsake, girl!

JACKIE. Billy! Billy!

She exits pursued by POLICEMEN.

LEN (*aside*). The Dimmocks. Always a law unto themselves.

Blackout.

Scene Four

Chorus: Staff of the Bunker. All Women

CHORUS.
> We are the workers at the centre
> We are the eyes of the nation
>
> This is the bunker
> Min. of Aircraft Production
> London
>
> This is the Ops Room in the Bunker
> Min. of Aircraft Production
> London
>
> We work the great map
>
> Linked to the other Ops Rooms
> Sector, Group and Fighter Command
>
> The great maps all in harmony
>
> Red for enemy
> Black for friendly
> Number to show height

Number to show strength
Arrow to indicate direction
Colour markings for each raid

We are the eyes of the nation

   Eight-hour shifts
            Morning afternoon night

Round the clock
   Never let your mind wander

Never let up or you're lost
People take pills people break

Never let up or you're lost
We are the eyes of the nation

   All around the room a balcony
   The commanders, looking down

We move the enemy bombers
We move our fighters

The commanders looking down, dead-eyed, dead-faced

We are the eyes of the nation
We too see how near we are
To catastrophe

Scene Five

Whitehall bunker.

LORD BEAVERBROOK – 'MAX' – *enters. Sixty-one years, Canadian accent. He carries a phone, trailing its wire. With him are young* MEN *and* WOMEN ASSISTANTS. *Some carry telephones on long lines that snake and tangle across the stage. Others carry clipboards and papers. They swarm about him. The phones are constantly ringing.*

BEAVERBROOK (*aside*). And this is my world. The Ministry of Aircraft Production. Whitehall. Underground. Everything slapped together, improvisation the order of the day, sealing wax and string. (*Into the phone.*) Well, how damn bad is it? If I don't know how bad things are I've not got a hell's chance of making them better! (*A beat.*) Do not try Britisher waffle on me, I want damage assessment at Supermarine's Woolston factory, in detail, now! (*A beat.*) Oh, the Southampton Post Office has been hit? Jerry bombed the phone lines. (*Cod-English.*) Hey-ho, chaps, how jolly unsporting of the Hun! (*Very loud.*) I am not the Minister for Phones I am the Minister for Aircraft Production, I don't care how just get me damage assessment on the factory and get me it NOW!

He slams the phone into its cradle. A new one is handed to him.

(*Listens, increasingly irritable.*) I do not know the damage assessment, Prime Minister, but I'll kick up a lulu of a kerfuffle to get it. (*A beat.*) I know we must know how bad things are if we're going to make them better! Hell in a bucket, Winston! What do you want me to do, walk on water?

LEN GOOCH *rides on to the stage on a bicycle. He jumps off it and exits, the bicycle left on the stage, a wheel spinning.*

(*A beat.*) Okay, I will be Jesus Christ and get Woolston working again! And one way or another I'll have a damage assessment – (*A beat.*) Yes, I will bring it to The Ritz tonight. Thank you for chewing only half my arse off.

Churchill has cracked a joke, e.g. 'Canadian rump is entirely inedible'. BEAVERBROOK *laughs.*

Yeah, Canadian backsides can be tough. Wash me down with the bubbly tonight. Thank you, Prime Minister.

He replaces the receiver and hands it to an ASSISTANT.

(*Aside*.) The worse the day, the longer the night with Winston at The Ritz. I'll be seeing the dawn in again. Dickered. (*To the* ASSISTANT.) What's going to get me first, the German Luftwaffe or my liver?

But he turns away before the ASSISTANT *can answer, as another* ASSISTANT *holds out a telephone to him.*

ASSISTANT. Minister, the Chief Engineer from the Woolston factory is telephoning.

BEAVERBROOK *grabs the telephone.*

BEAVERBROOK. Gooch, that you?

Revealed: LEN *on the telephone, an anxious woman,* MRS THORPE, *beside him.*

LEN. I must talk directly to Lord Beaverbrook.

BEAVERBROOK. You are. But how? Aren't the phones down?

LEN. In the town, yes, but I've cycled out to Hedge End. It's on a country exchange –

BEAVERBROOK. So this line is not secure?

LEN. No, it's a private house, I knocked them up –

BEAVERBROOK. And you've come direct from Woolston?

LEN. Yes yes, that's why I'm ringing –

BEAVERBROOK (*to the* ASSISTANT). The line's not scrambled. What do you think? (*Before the* ASSISTANT *can reply.*) Hell, make sure you're not overheard then give.

LEN. Mrs Thorpe, thank you so much for your help. But it's a national emergency call, so –

MRS THORPE. Would you like a cup of tea? When you're done?

LEN *stares at her for a moment, not able to take that in.*

LEN. Yes, yes, thank you very much.

MRS THORPE. But the cat got out, I must get him if you don't mind.

LEN. Right.

She exits.

BEAVERBROOK. Gooch, you there?

LEN. Yes.

BEAVERBROOK. Spill, spill –

LEN. It's all a hell of a mess, the roof's gone, the building's unsafe. One of the metal presses is smashed to bits. Five of the big jigs are knocked about a bit, most of the tools are intact.

BEAVERBROOK. The machine tools are intact?

LEN. Repairable or not touched.

A beat.

It's a miracle.

BEAVERBROOK. The trick is not to look down at the water.

LEN. Sorry?

BEAVERBROOK. Just being God, all part of the job. So we can get back into production –

LEN. It's the factory itself, Minister, it's all but gone. And even if we rush rebuilding –

BEAVERBROOK. – Jerry knows where you are and will be back. (*A beat.*) Well, the first thing is a detailed damage assessment to the machines –

LEN, *taking crumpled sheets of paper from inside his jacket.*

And AIR CHIEF MARSHAL DOWDING *enters, unremarked.*

LEN. Actually I've made one. Can you get a despatch rider down or shall I –

BEAVERBROOK. No, I'll hand you over to one of my people. Do it on the phone now then I can take it to The Ritz.

LEN. To – ?

BEAVERBROOK. Never mind. Good job, Gooch. Speak very soon.

LEN *turns away upstage and begins, unheard, to read details into the phone.*

An ASSISTANT *with a headset phone – wire trailing – writes what he says onto paper on a clipboard. This continues as* BEAVERBROOK *turns to* DOWDING.

Oh, Hugh.

DOWDING. I thought I'd come over.

BEAVERBROOK *turns to the* ASSISTANTS.

BEAVERBROOK. Thank you, all, I want to talk to the Air Chief Marshal.

They all exit, pulling lines, except for the ASSISTANT *who is taking notes from* LEN *on the telephone.*

DOWDING *is a secretly sensitive, intensely reserved man. His nickname used behind his back is 'Stuffy'. He is a brilliant commander.* BEAVERBROOK, *the opposite in temperament, is very fond of him.*

A beat.

How can I help?

DOWDING. I've come over about Woolston. How bad is it?

BEAVERBROOK. A detailed inventory's being phoned through now.

DOWDING. Someone got through? The lines to my obs people are all down.

BEAVERBROOK. Oh, a man with a spark of gumption got on a bike. It looks like the building is badly damaged. But most of the machine tools are intact.

DOWDING. The machines are intact?

BEAVERBROOK. By some kind of fluke. Or miracle.

DOWDING. I don't believe in miracles.

BEAVERBROOK. Nor do I. Except when I publish them in the *Daily Express*.

He laughs. DOWDING *is deadpan.*

DOWDING. Of course, now the Germans have pinpointed the position of the factory, if you rebuild they will bomb again at once.

BEAVERBROOK. Absolutely.

DOWDING. So perhaps you –

BEAVERBROOK. Perhaps I should move the machines. But where to? The only other place big enough is a hanger at Eastleigh Airfield, but a production factory on an airfield? Too risky.

DOWDING. Well, that is your problem. Mine is that, the last eight weeks, I have four hundred and eighty-nine Spitfires and Hurricanes badly damaged and in need of repair, and seven hundred and eighty-five totally lost. We are losing too many, Max. If you do not increase repair and replacement, we will go under.

BEAVERBROOK. I will get Woolston back on stream one way or another.

DOWDING. Good, then.

DOWDING *stands there, stiff, inert.*

A pause.

BEAVERBROOK. How are you bearing up, Hugh?

DOWDING. I don't really see the point of asking myself that.

BEAVERBROOK. No you don't, do you. Look, come with me to The Ritz tonight, talk to Winston.

DOWDING. I don't think so.

BEAVERBROOK. You've got to do the politics, Hugh. I watch your back best I can but you've got to do some infighting. You have enemies.

DOWDING. Yes. Hermann Göring for one.

BEAVERBROOK. Come to The Ritz, man!

DOWDING. I'm driving up to Bentley Priory.

BEAVERBROOK. The table at Fighter Command HQ, with incoming bombers, rather than a table at The Ritz with incoming bottles of champagne?

DOWDING. We all have our field of operations.

BEAVERBROOK. Good God! Was that wit?

DOWDING. No, profound disapproval. Please give my best wishes to Winston. And telephone me at the Priory if there is anything new from Woolston. Goodnight, Max.

BEAVERBROOK. Goodnight, Hugh.

DOWDING turns to go but stops.

DOWDING. I do appreciate your friendship.

BEAVERBROOK. And I yours.

DOWDING exits.

LEN finishes the conversation, and replaces the receiver in its cradle.

The ASSISTANT who has been taking notes from him runs to BEAVERBROOK and hands him the clipboard. He immediately begins to study it. ASSISTANTS cluster around him.

LEN *(calling into the night)*. Mrs Thorpe? Are you there? I should be getting on –

Enter MRS THORPE, carrying a cat in her arms.

MRS THORPE. It's all right, I found him. He's called Max, after Lord Beaverbrook. Say hello to him.

For a moment LEN is fazed.

LEN. Hello, Max.

For a moment LEN and the cat stare at each other.

BEAVERBROOK. Bollocks to buildings, I know what to do! I'm going to turn Southampton inside out!

He slaps the clipboard into the chest of an ASSISTANT.

Scene Six

Dimmock's Laundry.

FRED DIMMOCK *and* LEN GOOCH.

FRED *holds a valve*.

LEN (*aside*). Fred Dimmock, known him since we were nippers, almost a big brother to me.

FRED (*aside*). Bloody valve gone, water all over. Not bomb damage, who needs that when everything's falling apart anyway?

LEN (*aside*). Laundry. Never understood how the Dimmocks put up with the smell, sort of sour, off the dirty sheets and whatnot.

FRED (*aside*). I do love it so, the smell o' my business, warm, sort of cottony, the whiff of starchy linen at the end of a long day. And the look of it… big brown boilers, all shiny, big spinners six foot across, big brassy tumble dryers. It may be a little empire but it's all mine.

LEN (*aside*). But Official Secrets Act. Something I can't tell him and it's creasing me up.

A beat, then the scene begins.

FRED. Len, good of you to look in, given what you must be going through –

LEN. Just wanted to make sure you're all –

FRED. We're, we're fine. (*A beat.*) How bad?

LEN. Well, they finally hit us.

FRED. Not for want of trying. When they missed and hit the shelters over the road I thought –

LEN. Didn't we all.

A moment.

Well, there's a lot of damage, the roof's gone, half the office. But by some kind of miracle most of the machine tools are okay.

FRED. So how many – ?

LEN. With the workers in the shelters two days back – all in all, a hundred.

FRED. Dear God.

LEN. Joe Watson was there.

FRED. Annie and their little boy, I'll go round –

LEN. I've just been. Best leave it.

FRED. What we going to do, Len?

LEN. The obvious, Fred.

FRED. Grin, bear, carry on, and all that nonsense?

LEN. What else?

FRED. Could get it over with and surrender.

An odd moment. Then they laugh.

Carry on it is then.

He holds up the valve.

This valve's off my number-two boiler. The safety governor blew up, pop, just about hit the roof! I've got a mountain of dirty long johns, shirts, sheets, knickers of all kinds piling up. I need all the boilers on song, all the time. Give us a butcher's?

FRED *holds out the valve,* LEN *takes it reluctantly.*

LEN. Oh, give it here.

He looks at it.

There's a stress fracture. It's distorted the ball chamber.

FRED. Is it buggered?

LEN. Absolutely. You're lucky the governor on the boiler worked, the whole caboodle could have blown. As you bloody well know, Fred Dimmock. You can't run your machines down like this.

FRED. No choice! Where do I get spare parts? There's a war on.

LEN. I have noticed.

FRED *looks at him. A moment.*

No, no, no.

FRED. You've done little jobs for us before.

LEN. The factory's just been hit by God knows how many enemy planes!

FRED. But you said the machine tools are okay, this'll just take a small hand jig, when the power's back on, can't you –

LEN. Woolston's a bomb site!

FRED. I'm staring at bankruptcy here! My family could end up with the hobos on the Common.

LEN. And I could end up in jail.

FRED. For us?

LEN *hesitates.*

LEN. It's a big security clamp-down, the army all over –

FRED. Nah, squaddies, they don't know squat. They'll just see the Chief Engineer bent over a machine making a few sparks – Look, I know we're just a laundry, but keeping people's clothes clean, that's as much essential war work as making bloody Spitfires.

LEN. Is it?

FRED. Course! Morale! A bit of a stiff collar come a Friday night for one of our boys on leave, a nice crisp white blouse for his girl. We've got to keep clean, keep smart. When you put on clean underpants you know you're going to win. Yes, this laundry is on the home front.

LEN. God, Fred, you could talk Hitler into a game of cricket. (*A beat.*) Oh all right, give it here.

FRED. Bless you. Saved us. (*A beat.*) Look I've got a new batch of you-know-what.

LEN. You've made more?

FRED. Best yet. We'll need something strong to drink when we're fighting in the hills.

LEN. Fred, watch the defeatist talk.

FRED. Off-the-cuff, light-hearted remark, still a free country, in't it, technically? Look, just have a couple of bottles.

LEN. I think I'll pass, after that last lot.

FRED. Why, what was wrong with it?

LEN. The feeling you were going blind, for a start.

FRED. Château Dimmock is widely sought after.

LEN. Fred, I'm serious. Drinking in the town's getting out of hand. Jesus Christ, you're Chairman of the Chamber of Commerce! They find you selling illegal stuff, the proverbial ton of bricks'll come down.

FRED. It's just a bit of fun. Remember fun?

LEN. I think I do. From years ago. Some kind of dance craze, wan't it?

FRED laughs but LEN is not.

FRED. Len, is everything all right?

LEN. Can I give you a bit of advice? Be prepared.

FRED. What, we in the Boy Scouts now?

LEN. No, we're on the front line. The front line, Fred! If you don't know that, right through you, heart and mind, you are in deep trouble.

A pause.

FRED. What you trying to tell me?

They are staring at each other.

What? What, man?

Enter LILIAN DIMMOCK (forty-seven years). She carries a glass flagon.

LIL. Oh, Len, you're all right, thank God, it must be all sixes and sevens at Woolston.

LEN. Sixes and sevens about covers it.

LIL. Were many –

FRED, *a sharp shake of the head to* LEN.

LEN. We don't know yet.

LIL. It's selfish, but it's the people you know you fear for the most.

LEN. Yes.

FRED. Len's going to do us a new valve for the big boiler.

LIL. You can do that, after the bombing?

LEN. When your husband decides to twist an arm –

LIL (*lowers voice*). How about a couple of pounds of butter?

FRED. On the quiet.

LEN. 'Quiet' butter –

LIL. My cousin Ted's farm outside Weybridge, they've not ploughed up all his grass, he's still got a bit of a dairy herd. And – well, family first.

LEN. That what comes first? Family?

LIL. Course! What else we fighting for?

LEN. How you two hunt together!

FRED. That's cos we're the spice of life, in't we, Lil.

LIL. That's us. Nutmeg all over anything.

LEN. Keep the butter. (*Hesitates, then.*) I must be going.

FRED. Bless you, Len.

LEN (*to* FRED). Just remember what I said.

He exits. LIL *sags, puts the flagon down.*

FRED. You all right, old girl?

LIL. I don't feel spicy.

FRED. Well, it was a very heavy raid.

LIL. Fred, some nights maybe we should go up the Common.

FRED. No! I'm not doing that.

LIL. Just to feel safe.

FRED. Come Hitler or high water I am not leaving this laundry.

LIL. It's only machines 'n' washing powder!

FRED. Lil, no, please, old girl, no more talk of this.

She regroups.

LIL. What did Len want you to remember?

FRED. He dropped some kind of hint.

LIL. 'Bout what?

FRED. Couldn't read it. Something official. He's changed.

LIL. Change in't the half of it, round here.

Enter MARY 'MA' DIMMOCK.

MA. And is Len Gooch going to save our bacon and get this place back earning?

FRED. Yes, Ma.

He looks at LIL, *worried.*

LIL *(aside)*. When the war began I thought it would be a bomb coming through the roof. Not my mother-in-law.

MA. Well?

FRED. All in hand, Ma.

MA. He'll make a new valve on the QT, despite the raid?

FRED. All in hand.

MA. I was right to get you to ask him then.

FRED. You were indeed, Ma.

MA. Good to get credit for something round here. What he want in exchange?

FRED. Nothing.

MA. Nothing?

LIL. I offered him some of Ted's butter.

MA. Well, that is fishy.

LIL. Why fishy?

MA. There's something behind it.

LIL. He's doing it out of the goodness of his heart.

MA. Lilian, you trust too much. One thing I've learnt in this life: if there is a thing, there is a thing behind it.

I mean – (*Eyes* LIL *up and down*.) He's a lonely man, Len Gooch. All work, work. Definitely the type.

LIL. What type?

MA. Type to have a crush on an older woman.

LIL. Oh.

FRED. Ma, stop this.

MA. I'm just saying it's useful to have a man like Len Gooch on a string. If I've –

LIL. If you've learnt anything in this life, yes yes! And have you? Like just how you've got a steel point on the end of that nose, poking it into everything?

A beat.

MA. Well, there's no need to take that tone and I'm sorry you feel you have to.

LIL. Oh, I'm sorry, Ma –

MA. I've got a carrot roll in the range. I do have my uses.

LIL. Oh, please don't –

But MA *exits*.

Why is it always my fault?

FRED. Nothing's anyone's fault. Or everything's everyone's fault, I dunno.

LIL. I mean, she's taken over the cooking and is going to poison us all.

FRED. Her carrot roll's not bad.

LIL. It's horrible!

FRED. All right, yeah, it's horrendous.

He laughs, she does not.

LIL. What's happening to us, Fred?

FRED. We're doing our best.

LIL. Pity it's not good enough.

A pause.

FRED. I've got a thousand things.

LIL. Me too.

They are looking at each other, not knowing what to say, what to do.

Maybe – if you put HP Sauce on her carrot roll.

FRED. Need a big splash.

LIL. She'd hate us doing it.

FRED. Just pour it all over and sit out the row.

LIL. Shall we have a drink?

FRED. Is that a good idea?

LIL. We tested it last night and we're still here.

FRED. Hair-curling stuff, though. One of my best.

LIL. Didn't make me sleep, though.

Enter JACKIE.

JACKIE. What's for tea tonight? My rabbit?

LIL. I've chucked it.

JACKIE. What you mean, chucked it?

FRED. Good bit of poaching, Lil! Why you do that?

LIL. That rabbit belongs to Lady Cooper.

JACKIE. But it's dead.

LIL. It's still someone else's property.

JACKIE. Why should dead things belong to anyone?

LIL. I don't know, dear, maybe it's in the Bible.

FRED. There are bunnies running about all over up there. And there was that Min. of Ag notice saying shoot rabbits.

LIL. But not other people's! Oh, why do I worry?

FRED. Cos you're a good person, Lil. Just too good sometimes.

JACKIE. Actually she let us have it, she doesn't care.

LIL. You spoke to her ladyship?

JACKIE. Yeah.

LIL. And?

JACKIE. She came over as a bit of a sweetheart.

FRED. Wonder if she'd be a sweetheart if we took a deer!
    Venison, think of the price we'd get for that.

    MA *enters carrying the rabbit.*

MA. Who put this in the bin?

FRED. Oh no.

MA. This is fresh. Can't throw good meat away!

LIL. It's not ours.

JACKIE. Cos of the Bible.

MA. Well, it'll be ours if we eat it.

LIL. All right! Just ignore me! Undo everything I do!

    A beat.

JACKIE. Mum, sorry, it really don't matter.

    LIL *calms down.*

LIL. I know, I know, I'm being silly. I'll make us a pie.

MA. Actually a stew will go further and I've got carrots left over.

LIL. I'll do my pie with herbs.

MA. I don't hold with herbs, they're foreign.

JACKIE. Billy loves a pie.

    They look at her. A pause.

What men don't?

    A pause.

Yeah, what is it about men and pies?

FRED. Men like pies cos they mean England. Who is Billy?

JACKIE. The man I'm going to marry.

A silence. All staring at her.

FRED. The man you are going to what?

JACKIE. You heard, Dad.

A pause.

LIL. Oh, Jackie –

MA. Here we go.

LIL. You didn't tell us this was going on.

MA. I have smelt this, I have.

LIL. Why didn't you tell?

JACKIE. I'm telling now.

MA. Had a whiff of something not right!

JACKIE. I thought he'd died in the raid. But he hadn't. I asked him to marry me. Since he wan't dead.

MA. You asked him?

JACKIE. The world's changing, Gran.

MA. Yes but we don't have to.

FRED. Well, I'm sort of pleased, but you know, I'm your dad, I'd have thought you'd have asked.

JACKIE. Oh you want Billy to come round in his best uniform, doff his cap, ask your permission?

FRED. Why not! You are very precious to me.

JACKIE. That is so old-fashioned.

FRED. I am an old-fashioned bloke.

MA. Just because there's a war, young women think they can go off with minds of their own. It's unnatural.

LIL. Oh, why can't things be simple and – nice.

JACKIE. It will be more than nice, Mum, it will be wonderful, and gorgeous. (*To* MA.) And I'm not going off anywhere. I'm getting married, here.

A pause.

FRED. This Billy got a second name?

JACKIE. Lewis, Billy Lewis.

MA. Lewis.

FRED. Why was he in the raid?

JACKIE. He's a gunner.

LIL. A gunner, well.

JACKIE. He's with the machine-gun unit at Woolston's. In the raid they think they hit a Junkers.

FRED. But the unit was on the roof.

JACKIE. Yeah, it was a miracle. There was a girder, 'stead of falling he sort of – slid.

FRED. What about his mates?

JACKIE. One's very bad with his legs, the other's got concussion and broked-up ribs. Billy feels bad cos he's not touched.

FRED. Lad with a good heart?

JACKIE. I think so.

FRED. Sounds like he's the apple of your eye.

JACKIE. He is kind of lovely.

LIL. You've landed yourself a hero.

MA. Where's this Billy from?

JACKIE. Portsmouth.

Shock.

MA. Oh, my waters, I knew it! Lewis is a very Pompey name.

FRED. My daughter is going with a Pompeyite?

MA. My granddaughter – with scum?

JACKIE. He's not real Pompey, not Fratton or anything, he's from North End.

FRED. North End is still Portsmouth.

LIL (*to* JACKIE). It is, dear.

MA. A mixed marriage. In our family.

FRED. I'm not having a Pompeyite getting his feet under my table, I am not.

An air-raid siren starts up.

LIL. Maybe we'll keep it quiet.

FRED. Fat chance of that. You know how they shoot their mouths off.

MA. They think they're tops but let their children be mudlarks.

JACKIE. This is stupid! We're fighting a war together.

FRED. There are other wars going on!

JACKIE. What, doing down Pompey matters more than doing down Hitler?

MA. Your father's right, if we don't keep up standards what's the point of fighting Hitler?

FRED. It's what's close to home that matters!

A loud explosion a distance away. They freeze.

LIL. There! There! Close enough for you?

FRED. They're going for the docks now. Right, shelter! Family row after the all-clear.

They exit.

The siren goes to the all-clear.

Enter POLLY.

POLLY (*aside*). After a raid you come out the shelter, dead scared. But today I've got the most wonderful feeling in the world – I'm alive. Alive and I know something!

Supermarine have told us what Lord Beaverbrook's going to do. At school some girls jeered at me for being a loner, loving maths and drawing – Not that I cared. And look at me now – Polly Stride, Top Secret! Oh Jackie, going on about your soldier boy – I want to take hold of you, shake you, tell you. But then – oh is this awful of me – I love the feeling of being on the inside, knowing what others don't. Even my best friend. Yes, awful! When everything's going to be so exciting.

She laughs and exits.

Scene Seven

Hursley House.

LEN *and* LORD BEAVERBROOK. *A pompous, overweight* SERVANT, *in a pink uniform, bows to them and exits, trailing clouds of disdain.*

They look about them, seeing splendours.

A pause.

BEAVERBROOK. She all alone in this pile?

LEN. I think so, yes. There are the servants, of course.

BEAVERBROOK. The English aristo, to the manner accustomed.

LEN. Actually her husband, Sir George, passed away early this year.

BEAVERBROOK. Will that make things tricky?

LEN. They say she's staying put. Sounds a woman who knows her own mind.

BEAVERBROOK. We'll see about that. (*A beat.*) So they've hit the docks?

LEN. The town's a mess.

BEAVERBROOK. It's a goddamn mess all over. But that's what we've got. Make mess creative! Ha! How many rooms are there here?

LEN. According to Land Registry, fifty-seven.

BEAVERBROOK. You've researched the place already?

LEN. You get on with it.

BEAVERBROOK. Only way, Len. Do everything at once. You and I are going to see eye to eye.

LEN. I hope so, my lord.

BEAVERBROOK. Minister, that's what I am, just a minister.

LEN. Yes, sir.

BEAVERBROOK. When I was just a newspaper owner, people said I had power without responsibility. Now I have responsibility without power.

LEN. I wouldn't say that, sir.

BEAVERBROOK. You don't know the half of it. It's so damned ramshackle, so rickety, so fragile – state power. I never realised that, when I was on the outside.

I –

BEAVERBROOK *closes down for a moment*. LEN *is at a loss*.

LEN. That fellow dressed up as a prawn was something else. That look he gave us.

BEAVERBOOK *lights up again at once*.

BEAVERBROOK. All servants are snobs.

LEN. I think he had me down as a plumber.

BEAVERBROOK. In a kind of way, you are. (*Laughs*.) Me he saw as a colonial barbarian, come to wreck his world. Which I have.

He takes out a pocket watch.

Come on, come on, what are they doing, leaving us high and dry here?

A beat.

LEN. Actually Lady Cooper is American.

BEAVERBROOK. God spare me, what am I walking into, a Henry James novel?

LEN. Henry –

BEAVERBROOK. Wrote one story over and over. English aristo snaps up American heiress. He finds he really loves her, she finds she's dying of TB. This woman healthy?

LEN. I've no idea.

BEAVERBROOK. You know what we're going to do here is brutal. I hope you're up for it.

LEN *can't find a reply, and* SYLVIA *enters.*

SYLVIA. Lord Beaverbrook, so delighted to meet you. And you, sir, are –

LEN. Gooch.

SYLVIA. A great pleasure to meet you too, Mr Gooch.

LEN. Likewise.

BEAVERBROOK. My lady, I –

SYLVIA. Oh no, I'm not her ladyship. Goodness! I am a mere dogsbody. Lady Cooper does apologise, parking you, as it were. She and I have been in the stables.

BEAVERBROOK. You have horses?

SYLVIA. Marrows.

BEAVERBROOK. That a kind of pony?

SYLVIA. Pony? Of course not. Vegetables.

BEAVERBROOK. Oh, veggies.

SYLVIA. Rhubarb too. The horses were requisitioned but they did leave behind – shall we say quantities of useful material. Moist manure, shade, ideal for succulents.

BEAVERBROOK. Right.

SYLVIA. Please do come up. Her ladyship is in the drawing room.

She gestures to them to follow and walks away. They follow.

BEAVERBROOK. Feel put in your place, Len?

LEN. Horribly.

BEAVERBROOK. It's a technique.

The three of them exit.

Beautiful armchairs are set.

Enter LADY COOPER.

LADY COOPER (*aside*). It's coming to the house at last. This horrible time. Like the Great War came, twenty years ago. I think of it as a big brute, a bear, dripping mud over the stair carpets from its wellingtons. (*A beat.*) And everything is – slow – Are bears slow animals, as they come towards you, arms wide, to squeeze the life out of you? Oh, what should I do, stand here with flowers in my arms, or arranging them in a vase? Turn and say, 'Oh, how delightful to meet you'?

Enter SYLVIA, BEAVERBROOK *and* LEN.

SYLVIA. My lady, this is Lord Beaverbrook and Mr Gooch.

LADY COOPER *turns.*

LADY COOPER. Oh, how delightful to meet you. My lord, Mr Gooch.

BEAVERBROOK. Lady Cooper, the delight is mine.

LEN. Yes.

LADY COOPER. Please.

A gesture. They sit, though SYLVIA *stands a little way off.*

BEAVERBROOK. I am here with a request.

LADY COOPER. Well, I expected you wanted something.

BEAVERBROOK. Yes. I –

LADY COOPER. I can offer you tea. Or perhaps something stronger? My late husband was very fond of a Highland malt.

BEAVERBROOK. We're just fine. And let me say I was very sorry to hear of the death of your husband. This is a time of sacrifice.

LADY COOPER. Oh, George didn't die because of the war. It was just in the order of things. And before the order of things, we have no choice.

BEAVERBROOK. I don't believe that, not for a second. Forgive me, I know you have had a loss, but no. We are the masters of our fate.

LADY COOPER. Well, you may be. (*A beat*.) Do you want it for a hospital?

BEAVERBROOK. I –

LADY COOPER. The house. You are here for the house?

SYLVIA. My lady, don't say anything you may re–

BEAVERBROOK (*interrupting* SYLVIA).Yes. We want the house.

LADY COOPER. We were a hospital for wounded soldiers in the last war, too. Did you know that?

BEAVERBROOK. No, ah. This is the thing –

LADY COOPER. First for wounded soldiers and, later on, for American airmen.

BEAVERBROOK *wants to speak but* LEN *is in there*.

LEN. You bought the first X-ray machine in the Southampton area.

LADY COOPER. We did, young man, sweet of you to know that. You must have been looking me up.

LEN. Well –

LADY COOPER (*to* BEAVERBROOK). A hospital again, will it be for the RAF?

LEN. It's not –

BEAVERBROOK. The Government doesn't want the house for a hospital, Lady Cooper.

LADY COOPER. No?

BEAVERBROOK. You do know the Woolston Spitfire factory was bombed.

LADY COOPER. Yes, so terrible. Were many hurt?

BEAVERBROOK. Thirty dead.

LADY COOPER. So you want us to take in the wounded? Well –

BEAVERBROOK. This is the thing, Lady Cooper. We are moving the Spitfire factory.

A silence.

SYLVIA. You want to move a *factory* into Hursley House? Into – the library? The Entertainment Hall? This room? Metal and sparks and noise, and oil and bits of metal all over the floors, and – workers in overalls with – grease on their boots and sweaty armpits, half of them, no doubt, drunk? What about all the panelling, the marquetry, the carpets and the plaster cherubs on the ceilings, chandeliers, you can't have cherubs and chandeliers over machines making aeroplanes! Well, I can tell you, Lord Beaverbrook and you, whoever you are, Lady Cooper will not stand for it!

LADY COOPER. Sylvia, please be quiet. (*A beat.*) Is that it, Lord Beaverbrook? You want to turn my home into a factory?

BEAVERBROOK. Not a factory. We are asking that you take in the design department.

SYLVIA. And how many people does that involve?

LEN. At the moment a hundred and fifty-eight, but it will expand.

SYLVIA. A hundred and fifty-eight!

LEN. It's a big operation. At Woolston we're developing new versions of the Spitfire all the time. The design teams work flat-out. It's very secret work, Lady Cooper. Along with the designers and the draughtsmen doing copy work on the plans, there will be an army unit for security.

SYLVIA. Oh, the army too, more boots –

LADY COOPER. Yes of course they can come.

A pause.

BEAVERBROOK. That is very generous of you, Lady Cooper.

SYLVIA. Well! I imagine it doesn't matter what her ladyship
says. I expect you have a piece of paper with you
requisitioning the house.

LADY COOPER. Of course they do, Sylvia. That's why they
look so shamefaced.

She laughs, so does BEAVERBROOK.

BEAVERBROOK. You're a very gracious woman.

LADY COOPER. Thank you, kind sir.

SYLVIA. Said Red Riding Hood to the wolf.

A sharp look at her from BEAVERBROOK.

BEAVERBROOK. Mr Leonard Gooch here is Chief Engineer
at Supermarine, he will organise the move. Please bring any
problems to him, any time.

LADY COOPER. So when will you –

LEN. We'll start converting the rooms tomorrow.

BEAVERBROOK. I understand there's an attic floor?

LADY COOPER. Yes –

BEAVERBROOK. Is it possible for you to move up there?

SYLVIA. You are a bully, Lord Beaverbrook!

BEAVERBROOK. Absolutely, ma'am. That is why the Prime
Minister gave me this job.

LADY COOPER. So I have to move?

LEN. Tonight.

SYLVIA. Outrageous!

LEN. I will send men up to help with your move. And we will
take up carpets, board up panelling to protect the walls,
move valuables, maybe into the basement –

LADY COOPER. Yes. Arrangements.

LEN takes out a buff envelope.

SYLVIA *gasps.*

LEN. I have to give you this. It's the requisition warrant. If you could sign it some time and –

LADY COOPER *takes the envelope.*

LADY COOPER. Gentlemen, please, I want you to know I'm delighted. I thought the house was going to die. Now it will be full of young people. We used to have parties, now we are having – well, a war! The planes are so beautiful.

BEAVERBROOK. And deadly. That's why we need 'em. Lots of 'em.

LADY COOPER. Well, thank you.

BEAVERBROOK. Ma'am. (*To* SYLVIA.) Ma'am.

BEAVERBROOK *and* LEN *are going.*

LADY COOPER. Just one thing.

They stop.

The design department is coming here, but where is the factory going to go?

BEAVERBROOK. I can't tell you that. Classified information.

LADY COOPER. Ah. Well.

LEN *and* BEAVERBROOK *exit.*

SYLVIA. You can fight this.

LADY COOPER. I don't want to. I was dreading the war coming to the house. I thought it would be a hospital, I couldn't face that again, suffering and death, young men mauled by the bear. But this is different. This is positive.

SYLVIA. Mary, it's not. I fear everything we know will disappear.

They turn away from each other.

LADY COOPER. I'm going to give them a special welcome.

SYLVIA. Under their boots. It'll all go under.

LADY COOPER. The flowers in the long greenhouse – I'll do something with flowers.

Scene Eight

Chorus: Polly and the Men

MEN *in suits with briefcases, T-squares and rolls of paper. Voices interspersed with chorus for all.*

CHORUS.
> Hursley House, here we come
> Better up there than in the town
> Trees and cows not city smells
>
> We are the designers
> The technical wizards
> The visionaries with drawing boards
> We're married to the job
> Our true love is a fighter aeroplane

> *Enter* POLLY. *She carries a suitcase.*

> Good morning, Miss Stride.

POLLY. Morning, gentlemen. Or should I say boys?

CHORUS.
> Say what you like, Polly
> > Please
> > > Yes

POLLY. And are we getting ready for life in the stately home?

CHORUS.
> Can't wait to move in
> Can't wait to get going
>
> (*Aside.*) The only woman on the team
> Bloody good at her job
> Fits in
> No problem at all

>   Great legs
>   Great hips
>   Great hair

> But we don't let her see we look

POLLY (*aside*). I was brought up to be proper. And there's nothing wrong with proper. And… I know they look. And sometimes I sneak a look back and think I'm one woman in a world of men and I love it! But I keep that secret. Cos our work is our true love.

CHORUS.
>   We do our work
>   That's all that matters
>   We keep our hands to ourselves

POLLY (*aside*). So all in all it's very proper.

> POLLY *joining in the* CHORUS.

CHORUS *and* POLLY.
>   We are the designers
>   The technical wizards
>   The visionaries with drawing boards
>   We're married to the job
>   Our true love is a fighter aeroplane.

Scene Nine

Laundry.

POLLY *and* JACKIE.

POLLY *with her suitcase*.

JACKIE. I thought you'd been avoiding me.

POLLY. No –

JACKIE. It something about me and Billy?

POLLY. No! It's just chaos at Supermarine.

JACKIE. I've had a load of bollocks about him here, I tell you.

POLLY. Oh, I'm sorry –

JACKIE. I mean the man I love and am going to marry he nearly gets killed, and what do they worry about? That he's from bloody Portsmouth! Tell you what, let's go up to Hursley House, have another picnic. I need to get out of this bloody town.

POLLY. I can't.

JACKIE. Not scared of her ladyship, are you?

POLLY. No, I – don't think we'll be allowed up there now.

JACKIE. Why not?

A beat.

POLLY. Can you look after this for me? They're clothes I won't need.

JACKIE. Course.

POLLY *puts the suitcase down.*

POLLY. Thanks so much.

JACKIE. So you're moving out of your mum's?

POLLY. Things are a bit up in the air.

JACKIE. That what this is about, you've had a row? Bet they don't like you having fun, having the pick of a load of men!

POLLY. It's not that at all!

JACKIE. Anyway, where you moving to?

POLLY. Supermarine have got me digs in Winchester.

JACKIE. Winchester. Posh! (*Laughs.*) Why there?

POLLY. Can't say.

JACKIE. State secrets, eh? Polly Stride, running the country!

POLLY. I've got to go.

She hesitates.

Have they spoken to your dad?

JACKIE. Have who?

POLLY. There's a bus, I can't be late.

JACKIE. Polly, you're all kinds of different, what is going on –

POLLY. They're turning things upside down. We've all just got to hold on, yes?

She turns away to leave as FRED *enters.*

FRED. Hello, Poll.

POLLY. Hello, Mr Dimmock.

FRED. Hanging around for tea?

POLLY. I can't.

POLLY *exits quickly.*

FRED. What's up with her?

JACKIE. Oh lately she's Lady Mystery. (*A beat.*) All right, Dad, spit it out.

FRED. What I said 'bout your Billy and Pompey, it were just a bad joke – but I don't want you going off married. I need you here.

JACKIE. You're a man in love with a laundry. Surprised you don't divorce Mum and marry one o' the boilers!

FRED. Don't you dare talk like that.

JACKIE. You don't care about us.

FRED. Not care? This place keeps us alive! The laundry is the family, the family is the laundry!

JACKIE. Great! Put us all in a spin dryer, squeeze the bloody life out of us! I am marrying Billy, so lump it!

Enter LIL *with the flagon.*

LIL. Are we happy now?

FRED. No we are not! All of a sudden I am the evil father!

JACKIE. There is a world outside this place, y'know. A whole big fat beautiful world!

FRED. He's a soldier, he got away with it in the Woolston raid but he'll die, any moment, and break your heart.

JACKIE *stares at him, then exits running.*

(*Aside*.) If only I could – fix feelings like a machine! Just get a spanner and –

A wrenching gesture.

LIL. Why do we have to row?

FRED. Sweetheart, it'll wash over. It'll have to, like everything else. Like the city getting bombed to smithereens. Wash over.

LIL. Yes.

A beat. She withdraws from him.

What if she can't bear not being with this boy?

FRED. Well then, she can't!

He exits.

Enter MA.

MA (*aside*). When it's all too much I never let others see. Just go in my room, shut the door and do my gnashing of teeth and railing. Then I come out and – be what I always am. (*To* LIL.) Are you all all right now?

LIL *stares at* MA, *and* FRED *enters at speed.*

FRED. Give me that.

He pulls the flagon from LIL *and exits.*

LIL. What we going to do, Ma?

MA. Get over it, Lil. What else are we on earth for, 'cept for getting over things?

Enter JACKIE.

Now, Jacqueline, I want you to take yourself in hand –

JACKIE (*interrupting*). There's someone here to see Dad.

Enter LEN *and* BEAVERBROOK, *who holds back. And behind him there are two uniformed* POLICEMEN.

FRED *comes on after them, unobserved.*

LEN. Mrs Dimmock, Lil, Jackie, I need to talk to Fred.

MA. I think he is drowning the family's sorrows.

LEN. It's urgent. Really urgent. This – is Lord Beaverbrook.

LIL. Oh, my sainted aunt.

BEAVERBROOK. It's great to meet you folks and the country is going to be very grateful.

LIL. Grateful?

LEN. We don't have much time and the minister's seeing a lot of people in the town tonight. We must talk to Fred.

LIL. Why, what's he done?

MA. Jacqueline, get your father, now!

FRED *steps forward.*

FRED. He's here.

LEN. Fred, this is Lord Beaverbrook.

FRED. Well. Down from on high, are we?

BEAVERBROOK. Mr –

LEN (*low*). Dimmock –

BEAVERBROOK. Dimmock. I need to speak to you alone. On a matter of great national importance.

LIL. Oh God, what we done?

A beat.

FRED. Family, out.

MA. I really think I –

FRED. Out, Ma!

A moment.

MA. Come on. Let the men mess up whatever it is they want to mess up.

MA, LIL *and* JACQUELINE *exit.*

BEAVERBROOK. I know you're an important man in this town, so I'll say this straight. The Government is about to requisition business properties for vital war work. Yours is one of them. I know it's a sudden shock, I know it will involve upheaval and sacrifice. But I also know you're a patriotic man and that you'll set an example.

A silence.

FRED. Vital war work. My oh my. (*A beat.*) Tell you what, as a patriotic man whose name you don't know. (*Shouts.*) Not in a million fucking years is the Government getting its hands on my laundry!

End of Act One.

ACT TWO

Scene One

Chorus: Fred and the Business Families

The mass of the chorus, the three family groups.

CHORUS.
>Requi – sodding – bloody – sition orders?
>Thirty-five businesses
>All over the town
>
>It's Government gone mad
>Trampling on our lives
>
>Fred, Fred, what we going to do?

FRED. I know but you won't like it.

CHORUS.
>Why so coy, Fred Dimmock
>Chamber of Commerce Chairman
>(*Whisper*.) Master Mason of the Lodge
>(*Loud*.) You've always been the bigmouth
>Southampton big shot
>Tell us what to do!

FRED. I said: you won't like it.

Family groups, waving papers.

CHORUS.
>Government's taking our garage
>Came round with coppers and all
>Clear out in twenty-four hours
>
>Same at Holly Brooks
>All our stock, get it out
>And all the fruit and veg and food at Botley's store
>
>Get rid

Build a Spit in our garage?
    Spit in our little ironmonger's?
        Spit in our corner food shop?

Full chorus.

It's Government gone mad
Trampling on our lives

So why so coy, Fred Dimmock
Chamber of Commerce Chairman
(*Whisper*.) Master Mason of the Lodge
(*Loud*.) You've always been the bigmouth
Southampton big shot
What we going to do?

All staring at him. A silence.

FRED. The big bully Beaverbrook. He came down to my
laundry. Told me the whole mad scheme. Stood there amongst
my boilers and dryers with a great big grin on his ugly mug!
Told me his ministry were grabbing the lot and Supermarine
were moving in, and how grateful the country was!

CHORUS.
    Fred, what did you say?

FRED. I said: we control our lives and livelihoods.

CHORUS.
    Lives and livelihoods.

FRED. Democracy!

CHORUS.
    Democracy!

FRED. So let's tell the big bully boys, the Beaverbrooks, get
your hands off us and our families. Cos we are England's
heart. Bugger 'em! Tear up the requisition orders, barricade
yourselves in, anything, don't let 'em rip out England's
heart. I tell you. I tell you as a lifelong Tory – it's enough to
make me join the bloody Labour Party!

Unease.

CHORUS.
Wouldn't go that far.

A silence. Family groups.

And we could lose the garage
Forever

The store
The shop

The requisition order says failure to comply
Fines. Prison sentence.

FRED. In't we free? In't this a democracy?

Two groups, answering each other.

CHORUS.
It's Government gone mad
But they've got emergency powers

They trample over us
But we've got to win

Whatever it takes
Even a touch of dictatorship

To win

In the end all you can do
One way or another
Is just get through

Sorry Fred
Sorry Fred

The war's like bad weather
Just sit it out, get through
One way or another
Build bunks in the shelter

The war's like bad weather

FRED. If you lot are the heart of England, rip it out! It's dead!

Scene Two

Hursley House.

Enter LADY COOPER, SYLVIA *and the* SERVANT. SYLVIA *and the* SERVANT *are carrying a large model of a Spitfire made of flowers. It has a stand behind it.*

LADY COOPER. We'll put it in the main hall –

SYLVIA. It'll bend!

LADY COOPER. Real Spitfires don't bend, neither will mine.

SYLVIA. It looks ridiculous.

LADY COOPER. Grey times need a splash of colour.

They place the model in the middle of the stage then stand back and look at it.

A pause.

(*Aside.*) When we had parties before the Great War, the really big parties, on the main table we'd have floral arrangements. Once we had a deer, one-third life-size, made of roses. It's nice to be reminded.

LEN *and* LORD BEAVERBROOK *enter at the front of a crowd carry drawing boards, rolls of plans, set squares, etc. They are all* MEN *except for* POLLY *at the back, who carries rolls of plans.*

They stop dead in front of the Spitfire, staring at it for a moment of awkward silence.

BEAVERBROOK. That is a splendid thing!

Relief. Everyone bursts into applause, delight, smiles, laughter, some dropping plans and set squares.

LADY COOPER. It's all of you who are splendid. Welcome to my home.

BEAVERBROOK. Thank you, Lady Cooper… And yes, the Spitfire is the greatest fighter aircraft ever built. (*Points at the model.*) Those graceful wings, that smooth fuselage, very pretty, no? But it's not a thing of beauty at all. It's a violent, ugly killer – and exactly what we need. The new designs you'll dream up will make it even deadlier. Your work will come out of the sun and send the enemy screaming down to hell. So let's get on with it.

Murmurs, movement to leave.

LADY COOPER. One thing, please? We have cleared the furniture from the Entertainment Hall, so you can move in right away. I do, though, ask you to be careful of the wood panelling, it goes back to Oliver Cromwell's day.

LEN. We are going to board up the walls, my lady.

LADY COOPER. Well, all very good then –

BEAVERBROOK. Okay, people!

They all begin to move off to exit.

BEAVERBROOK, *intimate, taking* LADY COOPER*'s hand.*

Unnoticed, POLLY *remains.*

I hear you had great parties here.

LADY COOPER. That was a long time ago, Lord Beaverbrook.

BEAVERBROOK. Max, please.

LADY COOPER. I'm Mary. When there's victory, I will throw the party of all parties.

BEAVERBROOK. I hope to be invited, Mary.

LADY COOPER. You may be. If you don't hurt the Cromwell panelling.

They smile at each other.

BEAVERBROOK *takes her hand and with a little bow, kisses it*

Then he exits quickly.

(*Aside.*) Oh dear. Why do I always like men who are utter cads?

SYLVIA. What shall we –

LADY COOPER. I don't think the minister approved.

SYLVIA. He said it was splendid.

LADY COOPER. The trick with men like that is not to hear what they say, but what they mean. Put it in the conservatory. We'll let the village church have the flowers.

SYLVIA and the SERVANT, *carrying the floral Spitfire off.*

(*Aside.*) I don't really mind if they do wreck the wooden panelling. It's just a wonderful feeling, everything changing, going inside out.

She turns to go. POLLY *intercepts her.*

POLLY. Lady Cooper, I came back to say sorry about the rabbit.

LADY COOPER. Rabbit?

POLLY. It was very rude of us.

She remembers.

LADY COOPER. Oh yes. Did it end up a pie, a stew, or did you just jug it?

POLLY. My friend's grandmother made it into a stew. It's just that now I'll be working here, I feel embarrassed.

LADY COOPER. Don't be, not at all. You're very sweet.

POLLY. Thank you very much, my lady.

POLLY *goes to exit.*

LADY COOPER. So you're the only woman at Supermarine designing Spitfires. Amongst all the men?

POLLY. Actually I'm not meant to –

LADY COOPER. Talk about it, no (*A beat.*) Come and have tea with me, after work. I'm in the apartment, right up the top.

POLLY *hesitates for a moment.*

POLLY. I –

But makes up her mind.

Yes. Thank you, I will.

LADY COOPER. Lovely.

POLLY *exits.*

(*Aside.*) All the world before her… I was like that once.

She exits and BEAVERBROOK *and* LEN *enter.*

POLLY *stops. She and* BEAVERBROOK *stare at each other for a moment.*

Then POLLY *exits quickly.*

BEAVERBROOK *turns to* LEN.

BEAVERBROOK. Make sure the old bat keeps her nose out of things.

LEN. Oh I'm sure –

BEAVERBROOK. I don't want flower arrangements all over the design offices. Geranium propellers in vases. Ban her from the main body of the house.

LEN. It is her home –

BEAVERBROOK. No it is not, it is a top-secret location run by my ministry. And telephone my office with a list of everyone on her staff. I'll get the spooks to run a security check.

LEN. I'm sure that's not –

BEAVERBROOK. Brutal, Len, remember? War is total or you lose. How are we doing in the town?

LEN *pauses for a moment.*

LEN. We've identified thirty-five premises and taken over six.

BEAVERBROOK. *Six?* In three days, that all?

LEN. There's resistance.

BEAVERBROOK. Resistance is what they do in France. There it's patriotism, here it's treason. Len – I need finished planes coming out of Southampton in three weeks' time!

LEN. But how?

BEAVERBROOK. I deal with 'why', 'how' is up to you, okay?

LEN. I feel like I'm carpet-bombing my own town.

BEAVERBROOK. Then get on with it before Jerry does the job. I'm back to London now. Telephone me when the thirty-five are active. Like yesterday? Good luck.

He walks away. Turns.

Who was the girl with the men?

LEN. Oh. Polly Stride, design office.

BEAVERBROOK. Great get-alongs.

LEN. Get-a-longs?

BEAVERBROOK. Legs. Where the hell is my driver?

He exits.

LEN *alone. He leans against a wall, lights a cigarette and smokes.*

LEN (*aside*). The breath of the beast on me, Beaverbrook's face always over my shoulder, that voice in my ear: more! Do more! More! I can't sleep. And when I do I have a nightmare. There's a door I've got to open, I get to it but the handle comes off. I wake up, terrified. But I'm still dreaming. At last I open the door, there's a huge room and – everyone's dead. (*A beat.*) Pull yourself together, Len. Oh, for coffee, real coffee!

Scene Three

Chorus: The Trekkers and Jackie

CHORUS.
> Southampton pride
> > Toughness from the sea
> > > Cheerfulness all round

> But sh sh – underneath
> Deep and lasting shock

> And now the night raids have begun

> Rumours
> > Gruesome stuff
> Rumours

> Fifty-thousand deaths a night
>> Martial law in Liverpool
>>> Trains from London full of dead

> Don't know what to believe
>> So when night-time comes

> Some of us lock up
> Carry what we can
> Go up on the Common
> Party with the Trekkers

Enter JACKIE, *dressed for a night out.*

> Let 'em bomb the house
> Life matters more than houses
> Life matters more than towns

JACKIE. Frantic, cars, vans, people getting out of the city,
   Billy, you're bloody late.

CHORUS.
> Come up the Common, darling
> Few bevvies round the bonfire
> Roll up snug till the morning –

JACKIE. Bugger off, my boyfriend's here. (*Waves.*) Billy!

CHORUS.
> Watch out, that car! THAT CAR!

JACKIE. Billy!

The CHORUS *freezes, horrified.* JACKIE *rushes forward,
stumbles, falls to the ground.*

Scene Four

Laundry.

FRED *has been drinking and is in a wild state.*

FRED. An Englishman in his castle – will never be denied. Never be denied, not till old Blighty's gone and died.

　LIL *enters, fast.*

LIL. Have you see Jackie?

FRED. No.

LIL. She's not come home all night.

FRED. Out on the tiles – and why not?

LIL. Oh dear.

　She exits.

FRED. Englishman's castle wall. In-preg-na-bull. British Bulldog one two three, British Bulldog one two three.

　LIL *enters yet again.*

LIL. Len – Len Gooch is here. And he's got – police.

FRED. Great! Let 'em come! I'll stick their heads on spikes, over my drawbridge!

LIL. Draw what, dear?

　LEN *enters. He carries a briefcase.* MA *enters unseen and overhears.*

LEN (*speaking, off*). No, wait.

FRED. I know what you're here for and no way is Beaverbrook getting his hands on my laundry!

LEN. You don't have a choice. It's vital war work.

FRED. I do vital war work.

LEN. Washing shirts?

FRED. Protecting what's mine! My dignity! My family!

LIL. Oh, what's happening to us?

　She exits.

LEN. Fred, I know it's hard –

FRED. Not hard at all! Just get out of my castle. Home.

LEN *steels himself.*

LEN. I've got a warrant.

FRED. A warrant, goodness.

LEN. Requisitioning these premises.

FRED. And what – chucking my family out on the street?

LEN. Supermarine will employ you as a general manager.

FRED. 'General manager'? Glorified office boy, more like – in my own premises!

LEN. You have expertise that –

FRED. You really are one of 'em now. A right Beaverbrook bully.

MA *comes forward.* LIL *enters.*

LEN. When will you people wake up to what is going on in this town?

MA. I am well awake, Leonard Gooch! Supermarine are taking over other laundries, like Dimmock's, and convenience stores that have a lot of space. And you're grabbing garages, they've got good power lines for the machines, like Austin House on the corner of Bannister Road. Word is, a shop on the Dukes Road to store finished parts. Hursley Road Stores will stockpile raw materials. Newton Works woodmill is where you'll do woodwork and metal assemblies. And then Spitfires will be put together at Eastleigh Airport.

They all stare at her.

A pause.

LEN. That is highly classified information! How did you –

MA. I'm a grandmother. Nothing happens in Southampton without the grannies knowing. No one notices us old dears sitting on a bench by the river having a natter, no one notices when we're in the room.

LIL. We notice when you're in the room, Ma –

MA. You're calling them shadow factories.

LEN. Then, Mrs Dimmock, you understand what we're trying to do.

MA. Too bloody right I do! So get your grubby, big Government hands off our family business!

LEN. Fred, I've got to warn you, kick against this and you'll go to jail.

FRED. Yeah, well, when the Nazis arrive what'll be the difference?

LEN. That's loose talk –

FRED. Yeah let's all go 'loose' as the bombs fall and Beaverbrook takes over our homes, our everything, 'loose' out on the Common, stormtroopers coming at us with torchlights through the trees!

LEN. Are you pissed?

MA. Of course he's pissed! Like everyone in this town trying to get through the day, let alone the night. Everyone's terrified, look at my daughter-in-law.

LIL. Thanks, Ma.

FRED. What you want to make here at Dimmock's anyway?

LEN. Can't tell you that till you sign the warrant.

MA. Typical bureaucrat, catching you every which ways!

LEN. I am not a bureaucrat, I am an engineer!

LIL. Oh, why must we row, why can't we just –

MA. All right, Mr Engineer, look around you. These boilers and dryers are for cleaning sheets, not making aeroplanes!

LEN. We'll move in machine tools from Woolston, your machines will be moved out.

FRED. What, scrapped?

LEN. You'll have to – find storage.

FRED. Tell you what you are – worse than one of them tinpot, would-be, Doctor Goebbels types on the BBC, telling us what to do!

MA. Too right, like the aluminium.

LEN. The what?

MA. That madcap Government scheme. Give us your pots and pans, we'll melt 'em down for aeroplanes. But you're chucking 'em all away, the aluminium's useless, too low-grade.

LEN. More granny information?

MA. You're burying our saucepans, frying pans in pits, all over the country. I bet there's one near Portsmouth.

LEN. You're talking twaddle!

MA. No, you are! Shadow factories? A fairy-tale made up to make us feel good while we get bombed to bits!

LEN. Supermarine is taking over Dimmock's Laundry and you will have to lump it. And I tell you, woman, wash the defeatist talk out of your mouth.

MA. What, or you'll turn me in?

Suddenly LIL *drops the flagon of hooch. It smashes. They all look at it.*

A pause.

LIL. That was the last peacetime one, brewed that lovely August.

LIL *points at the mess on the floor.*

See? The last good summer.

LEN, *taking out a warrant from his briefcase.*

LEN. I got no choice, nor have you. Here –

He holds out the warrant.

Sign the bloody thing, or God help me I'll have you arrested.

FRED. Got the power, have you?

LEN. It's not me that's got the power, it's England.

FRED. And what, you are England now? Not me, my family, the people of this town, all the towns, all the farms, the fishermen, the soldiers, the fire-watchers, the bobbies on their bikes in the country lanes, the mums, dads, kids, cities and villages – they're not England at all. People like you are, walking into homes with briefcases, policemen, soldiers with guns at your back.

A beat, the men staring at each other.

LEN. I'll be back at six. Tonight we'll rip out the laundry machines, have the Supermarine tools in by midday tomorrow. That's how it is. Lil, Mrs Dimmock.

He exits.

The three of them are still. A pause.

LIL. I'll clear that up, I will.

She exits.

FRED. What do we build up anything for, eh, Ma? It's all gone, plans, dreams. Everything that was hard and solid's turning to smoke. It's in your eyes, in your mouth, you can't see to walk through it – I am so – tired.

MA. Don't you go feeble on me, Fred Dimmock! Feeble like your father.

Enter LIL with a dustpan and brush.

LIL. I'll clear up, everything will be all right, it will.

Enter JACKIE, as from the street. She looks terrible.

Jackie, darling, what you gone and done to yourself?

JACKIE. I loved him but you never saw him. Cos you've all got Southampton stuck so far up your bums –

MA. Jacqueline Dimmock, no call for that talk.

JACKIE. We were going to elope. And yeah, Dad, live in Pompey! We were looking at a house, Liss Road in Fratton. And I'd never have spoken to you again, and you'd never have seen your grandkids either.

They stare at her.

LIL. Billy? What, he's thrown you up, or –

JACKIE. Or.

FRED. Oh dear God – was it last night's raid?

JACKIE. Not the raid. Accident. A stupid, crappy – can't say it, I –

She freezes. A moment, then she can continue.

He was knocked down by a car. A car! A soldier, on a night out, not in battle, not France, not fighting the Bosch coming up the beaches, not hit by a bullet – but by a car in Bugle Street.

LIL. Oh my lovely –

JACKIE. – And the streets, you know what they're like, evening, the blackout, everyone rushing to get out of the town cos of the night raids. But we were going the opposite way, a drink at The Duke of Wellington, a quiet dr– dr–

LIL. You don't have to tell –

JACKIE, *a flashback, seeing it.*

JACKIE. Taped-up headlights . And Billy's under the front o' the car, ten foot away, his leg sort of – wrong. Saw someone dead at Woolston, now I seen –

She freezes.

FRED. Give us a hug, love.

JACKIE. Bugger your hugs! You'd never have let Billy in, ever. I'm going to kip at Polly's. Don't come near me.

LIL. Please, when all's said and done we're your family.

JACKIE. Know what my family is now? A dead soldier. So treat me dead, too.

She exits. A slammed door.

MA. Chip off the old block there.

LIL. I'll go after her.

MA. Let her be. Grief's like flu, can't do anything about it but it passes.

FRED. You build things up, what for? Just to watch 'em be knocked down? Englishman's castle? (*Scoffs.*) Right, they want this place? They can have it. We're moving out.

LIL. Out to where, dear?

FRED. Treat us like the scum of the earth? Scum of the earth we'll be. A merry band, under the greenwood tree.

LIL. Tree, darling?

MA. He wants us to go trekking.

LIL. Oh. I dunno.

FRED. You said you wanted to, to be safe!

LIL. Yeah, but those people up on the Common? Maybe it won't be nice.

MA. There are hundreds up there these nights.

FRED. We'll get some peace of mind, and quiet, Lil. 'Way from bombs. It'll be like an holiday. As for this place? If Len Gooch can get heavy machine tools to run off this wiring, good luck to him.

MA. We could do a bit of business up in the trees, set up a still.

A pause.

LIL. I'd better look out the old tent.

Scene Five

Hursley House. LADY COOPER's flat. Sofa, small table.

JACKIE *and* POLLY. POLLY *is looking out*, JACKIE *is not*.

A silence.

POLLY. You can just see the sea from here.

> JACKIE *scoffs*.

> Oh look, there's a deer.

JACKIE. Oh a deer, 'jolly bloody hockey sticks'. It's a disgusting, stately home, the old bag with all that food running around – and down in the town good meat's black market, if you can get it.

POLLY. You thought she was a bit of a sweetie when we first met her.

JACKIE. Well, wrong, wan't I. Why you bring me here, Poll?

POLLY. I thought you should get out a bit.

JACKIE. You want me out of your digs, that it?

POLLY. No –

JACKIE. Where's the lav?

POLLY. I think it's thro–

> JACKIE *exits*.

> (*Aside.*) People go like that in the town, all the time. Because of the pain. I don't know how to help her.

> *Enter* LADY COOPER *with a tea tray*.

> Oh, let me –

LADY COOPER. It's okay.

> *She puts the tray down and looks around.*

> Where's –

POLLY. She's –

LADY COOPER. Ah.

POLLY. Let's start tea.

LADY COOPER. Very well.

A silence as LADY COOPER *pours tea. They sip, then –*

Is Jackie –

POLLY. Lots of people are drinking in the town, Mary. And up on the Common. Everyone's under terrible strain.

LADY COOPER. And how about you?

POLLY. What do you mean?

LADY COOPER. Being the only woman amongst the men, isn't that a strain?

A beat.

Sorry, I've been dying to ask.

POLLY. I'm very good at my job, they respect that.

A beat.

Though – When I go into the office, it is rather like walking on water – on a sea of men's secret glances.

LADY COOPER. How exciting. But it could be dangerous, Polly.

POLLY. I know what I'm doing. It's the work that matters.

They sip the tea.

And what about you? All these people, taking over your home?

LADY COOPER. I love it. (*A beat.*) No I don't. I wanted to help, even throw the odd party for you all. But they've cut me out, pushed me up here.

POLLY. It's secret work.

LADY COOPER. I do like being a bit of a Queen Bee. I think you do too.

POLLY. Do I? Oh dear.

They laugh. POLLY *makes up her mind to say –*

Jackie's fiancé was killed. In a car accident.

LADY COOPER. I see.

POLLY. I'm so worried about her.

JACKIE *enters. They look at her.*

JACKIE. Talking about me?

A beat.

LADY COOPER. It's kind of you to come and see me, Miss Dimmock. Jackie, I can call you Jackie?

JACKIE. Do what you like.

LADY COOPER. Polly told me what happened to your fiancé. I'm so very sorry.

JACKIE. Are you? My dad said we should shoot one of your deer.

LADY COOPER *puts the cup of tea down.*

LADY COOPER. Did he now.

JACKIE. Butcher it, flog it on the QT. Make a mint.

LADY COOPER. I'm sure people would find it delicious.

JACKIE. Bet it's all venison steaks for you, venison stew, venison sandwiches for tea.

LADY COOPER. We are all so obsessed with food.

JACKIE. Yeah, in't we! Come down to the town and live on a ration o' two ounces o' bacon a week!

POLLY. Jackie –

JACKIE. Don't you know what's going on where we live? Don't you see the smoke in the morning, hanging over the town? Rubble town. Oh, let's have tea up on the hill here, cock up our little fingers holding dainty little cups while we piss on the little people in their horrible little rubble holes, getting smashed to bits, blood and – blood and – all over the streets.

LADY COOPER, *standing.*

LADY COOPER. I have welcomed you into my house.

JACKIE. Oh yeah, big doll's house, you're – playing dolls up here, you're a doll, Lady Bountiful, playing at war. I hate you. Hate it. Hate hate hate hate –

LADY COOPER slaps her. JACKIE stares at her.

LADY COOPER. I lost someone, not long ago.

JACKIE. What, walking along the street?

LADY COOPER. No, months sitting by his bed watching him turn into a skeleton.

JACKIE hesitates. But she cannot connect.

JACKIE. I have to go.

LADY COOPER. Please don't –

But JACKIE exits, quickly.

POLLY. It's my fault, bringing her.

LADY COOPER. Don't be silly.

POLLY. I wanted to take her in the design office, show her what I do, interest her, but the guards wouldn't give her a pass.

LADY COOPER. Can't her family –

POLLY. They're not speaking. I've tried with her but –

LADY COOPER. Try again. (*A beat.*) Being a good person's a pain in the backside.

POLLY. That what I am, good? How boring.

LADY COOPER. Polly, the future belongs to girls like you.

POLLY. Don't know about that –

LADY COOPER. After the war it'll be your turn. You'll be able to do anything.

POLLY. You think so? Maybe it'll all just go back to normal.

LADY COOPER. It can't, not after all we're going through.

POLLY. Anyway, I think I'll still get drunk now and then.

LADY COOPER. Absolutely!

POLLY. I think with that Lionel, in the design office.

LADY COOPER. Take him down a peg or two?

POLLY. Why not?

They laugh. Enter SYLVIA.

SYLVIA. The Big Beast is here. Again.

LADY COOPER. Never rains but – Polly dear, quick. I don't want him to see me with a Supermarine worker. Through there, back stairs, wait on the little landing. And take the tea things. Three cups.

POLLY. I –

LADY COOPER. Do what I say, go!

But BEAVERBROOK *and* LEN *enter.*

Oh, Carruthers.

BEAVERBROOK (*to* POLLY). What are you doing here?

LADY COOPER. Miss Stride and I are taking tea.

BEAVERBROOK. 'Taking tea' builds no aeroplanes.

POLLY. I –

LEN. Polly, no.

A pause.

POLLY. Thank you for tea, Lady Cooper.

LADY COOPER. A pleasure, my dear, it was fun.

POLLY *exits.*

BEAVERBROOK. Mary, we have a situation.

LADY COOPER. A situation! More fun?

BEAVERBROOK. Not really. (*Turns to* LEN.)

LEN. Miss Meinster, there are two constables outside, please leave the premises with them.

A silence.

SYLVIA. I'm sorry?

LEN. You are excluded from Hursley House.

LADY COOPER. What do you mean, excluded?

LEN. Your effects will be sent after you once they have been examined.

SYLVIA. You mean my – what – clothes, my things?

LEN. I'm afraid so.

LADY COOPER. Are you inhuman?

LEN. We're all condemned to what we have to do.

LADY COOPER. Oh, piffle!

SYLVIA. What is it that I am meant to have done?

LEN. It's a matter of national security.

BEAVERBROOK. Nothing personal.

SYLVIA. Of course it's personal. It's my name. Meinster.

BEAVERBROOK (*low*). Len –

SYLVIA (*interrupting*). Meinster. German-sounding, is that it? You've gone through a list of names of people at the house and come up with mine, because it sounds German.

LEN. Don't let's have a scene, miss.

SYLVIA. What, are you going to intern me? Lock me up on the Isle of Man?

LEN. There's no question of internment, we've just been told you've been classified category 'C'. As a security risk.

SYLVIA. It's not even a German name, it's Dutch! Seventeenth century, my ancestor was a soldier. Fought with the English against the Spanish, married an English girl from Norwich. Mongrels! Mongrel nation, that's England! Maybe you should lock us all up!

A silence.

LEN. I'm sorry, Miss Meinster, but –

SYLVIA *exits quickly.*

LADY COOPER. This is outrageous –

BEAVERBROOK. And there's your butler.

LADY COOPER. Jameson?

BEAVERBROOK. He's got a criminal record.

LADY COOPER. What butler hasn't?

BEAVERBROOK. MI5 have decided your entire staff is a security risk.

LADY COOPER. You're getting rid of all my people?

BEAVERBROOK. Please see it as a request.

LADY COOPER. And not a boot kicking me in the face?

LEN. I'm sorry, Lady Coo–

LADY COOPER. Oh, shut up, you feeble man. (*To* BEAVERBROOK.) This is unjust.

BEAVERBROOK. I care about the big picture.

LADY COOPER. And not our little lives?

BEAVERBROOK. We face the obliteration of everything we know. So if some get mashed up on the long slog to a victory, so be it.

LADY COOPER. And I am duly mashed.

LEN. You just won't have any servants. We are all in this together.

LADY COOPER. Don't talk to me in propaganda clichés.

BEAVERBROOK. I hope we can still be friends.

LADY COOPER. Why not? I'm American, you're Canadian, we're both aliens in this country.

BEAVERBROOK. Cheap shot.

LADY COOPER. I want to be alone now.

BEAVERBROOK *and* LEN *exit.*

(*Aside*.) When brutes are kings. When beasts do feast. And we, under the table, are terrified of the dogs. (*Calls*.) Polly, did you wait? Polly!

Enter POLLY. LADY COOPER *turns away.*

POLLY. Mary, what's happened?

LADY COOPER. Beastliness. That's all. Beastliness.

POLLY. Can I –

LADY COOPER *turns to her.*

LADY COOPER. Can you get your friend back here tonight?

JACKIE. I can leave a message at the digs –

LADY COOPER. Good. I've got a wonderful idea.

A blackout.

Scene Six

Night. Outside Hursley House.

POLLY *is smoking nervously, looking for someone.*

POLLY. Oh, come on, come on.

Enter LORD BEAVERBROOK, *carrying a big briefcase, files under an arm. He sees* POLLY, *she does not see him.*

BEAVERBROOK. Miss Stride.

She starts.

POLLY. Oh –

BEAVERBROOK. Waiting for some lucky man?

POLLY. I was working late and missed the bus.

BEAVERBROOK. Your digs are in Winchester?

POLLY. Yes –

BEAVERBROOK. I'll drive you. How are the restaurants in wartime Winchester?

POLLY. That – that's very kind, but I've telephoned for a car from the pool.

BEAVERBROOK. Cancel it. My chariot awaits.

A moment.

POLLY. If you don't go straight to London, won't the Air
   Ministry fall apart?

BEAVERBROOK *laughs.*

BEAVERBROOK. You are sparky.

POLLY. Am I?

BEAVERBROOK. But what you say is very true. Goodnight,
   Miss Stride.

POLLY. Goodnight, sir.

   BEAVERBROOK *turns away.*

   At that moment, JACKIE *enters out of the darkness.* POLLY
   frantically waves her away.

   JACKIE *obeys.*

   BEAVERBROOK *turns back.*

BEAVERBROOK. This afternoon, breaking up the tea party.
   Sorry I was a grizzler.

POLLY. Grizzler?

BEAVERBROOK. Bear. We have bears in Canada.

POLLY. And are they rude too?

BEAVERBROOK. More sparky.

   POLLY, *turning away.*

POLLY. I think I should –

BEAVERBROOK. Mr Gooch speaks very highly of you.

   POLLY *stops.*

   I mean, there are no limits, if you're truly ambitious. Are you
   truly ambitious?

POLLY. I think you're being forward.

BEAVERBROOK. I'm from a forward race of men.

POLLY. Of bears, you mean.

BEAVERBROOK *laughs*.

BEAVERBROOK. Let's talk work. I've been thinking of the technical designs they send out to the shadow factories. They're going to have to be clear, we want engineers from all backgrounds. Hell, there's even a man who runs a laundry. How do we train him up in three days to make a bit of Spitfire?

POLLY. I think your laundry man's the father of a friend of mine. He won't take kindly to training. But –

BEAVERBROOK. But?

POLLY. If you think of the components as – kits. To be built in stages.

BEAVERBROOK. Like a kiddy's model?

POLLY. Yes.

BEAVERBROOK. I'll get on to that. Look, this weekend, I'll send a car to your digs, come up to London, we'll discuss it at the Ministry. And we could –

He smiles, a shrug.

POLLY. If you're going to say 'see the sights', I'll have to slap your face.

BEAVERBROOK. I hope that won't be necessary.

They are looking at each other, faint smiles.

He walks away and exits.

POLLY *is shaken.*

POLLY (*aside*). Slap his face! How could I say that? Go up to the London? He's a toad, a toad! (*A beat.*) I could work at the Ministry. But the toad. Do it. Can I?

JACKIE *comes out of the dark.*

JACKIE. Polly Stride, you are a deep one.

POLLY. What do you mean?

JACKIE. Getting your hooks into a high-up? Never have thought it!

POLLY. It's not that!

JACKIE. Course not. But if he gives you clothes, share 'em around.

POLLY. Shut up, Jackie, you don't have the faintest –

A torchlight light flashes.

That's her.

JACKIE. Why do you want me back up here, Polly?

POLLY. Told you, it's a surprise! Come on. She said we can get there through the conservatory.

JACKIE. Get where?

But POLLY *is off. They exit quickly.*

Scene Seven

Conservatory/corridor/design office. The stage is dark. POLLY *has a torch.*

Enter LADY COOPER *with a torch, the beam on the ground.*

LADY COOPER. Polly? Jackie?

POLLY, *turning on a torch.*

POLLY. Yes.

JACKIE. I'm not going to eat humble pie, just cos of this afternoon, you know –

LADY COOPER. No time for that, come on!

POLLY. How do we –

As if they are moving along a corridor.

LADY COOPER. It's an old servant way, from the conservatory, through the old kitchen, then the back stairs. And there's a door. I don't think they know it's there.

They stop.

A pause.

JACKIE. Where are we?

POLLY. Design office.

They move.

This is my drawing board.

She unrolls a blueprint.

And this is the design for the wing for the new high altitude version, Mk VII.

JACKIE. You made this?

POLLY. I drew it.

JACKIE. Yourself?

POLLY. Yes.

LADY COOPER. That is a thing of beauty.

JACKIE. What are these?

POLLY. Square tubes, see there are five of them, see, they fit into each other, like a box. And this Mk will have pointed wing tips.

JACKIE. So what's the secret?

POLLY. It's all secret.

JACKIE. No. What's the secret of making a plane fly?

POLLY. Oh! It's air pressure. The top of the wing's curved. It makes the air go faster over the top than the air underneath. So the pressure under the wing is stronger and – it lifts the plane up. Like this!

She picks up a sheet of paper, A4 size. LADY COOPER *takes* POLLY*'s torch.*

POLLY *holds the paper at its edge. She and* JACKIE *blow across it. It flutters up in the air.*

The three of them laugh.

JACKIE. That's magic.

POLLY. No, just natural forces.

A sound. They freeze.

LADY COOPER. Girls, go!

POLLY. But –

LEN (*unseen*). Who's in here?

LADY COOPER. Now!

Lights up. All still.

This was my idea.

POLLY. No it was mine.

JACKIE. It's me, I put 'em up to it.

LEN. Breaking into a restricted area? You know how serious this is?

JACKIE. Len Gooch, you still one of us?

LEN. What d'you mean?

JACKIE. You with us in the town? Or you really turned into what Dad says you are, a Government bully boy?

LEN. That is so bloody unfair –

JACKIE. I just wanted to see where Polly worked, that's all. So let us go.

LADY COOPER. I will take –

JACKIE (*to* LADY COOPER). Shut up. (*To* LEN.) You need Dad back at the laundry, don't you. Admit it.

LEN. It is a bloody mess down there. The wiring –

JACKIE. Let us off and I'll go up the Common with you, crack of dawn. Get him back.

LEN. I don't know if I –

JACKIE. You and Dad were friends. All of us, that close, our families, thick as thieves – oh, for fuck's sake, Len, let us go!

A pause.

LEN. Why do I feel well and truly Dimmocked? All right. Get out of here! All of you! Now.

JACKIE *and* POLLY *run for it, hand in hand. But* LADY COOPER *stands still.* JACKIE *and* POLLY *realise.*

POLLY. Mary?

LADY COOPER. One minute. Go on!

Exit JACKIE *and* POLLY.

I had my wedding breakfast in this room. I will not be told to get out of it.

LEN. My lady, I will have to call the guard post.

LADY COOPER. So be it. Call them. Call the men with guns, the Government. Take it all away from me!

Scene Eight

The Common, the South Coast of England, and the Filter Room at the Ministry of Aircraft Production.

On the Common, FRED, *sitting by the family possessions.*

The CHORUS *is divided into two.*

On the South Coast of England: CHORUS NO. 1 *as members of the Observer Corps. They wear metal helmets, warm clothing and carry binoculars.* CHORUS NO. 2 *are revealed as workers in the Filter Room with* LORD BEAVERBROOK *and two* SENIOR RAF OFFICERS *looking down on the map.*

CHORUS NO. 1.
    Sky-watchers
        Volunteers of the Royal Observer Corps
            Spotting enemy planes

    We do what the radar can't
        Radar points out to sea
            Once the Germans cross the coast
                It's down to us

FRED *(aside)*. The Common. A week of it, dew on your face in the morning, like iced water up your nose. All of us have got frozen feet and sniffles. And I han't got the tent up. There's a pole missing, there's got to be. And Lil – 'fraid her cold's going to turn worse. Why we come up here? Oh yeah, that was why. I'll have to go back. No I can't. I won't.

CHORUS NO. 1.
>It's down to us
>>They give us this little book

They all hold up a small book.

>Spotting German aircraft
>>Which we do
>>>Phoning in the numbers

>Straight to fighter high command
>>So the ops rooms know
>>>So the great maps work

>Hundreds of us
>>All along the coast
>>>All dead keen

They raise binoculars. They lower them.

>But what do we do on days of cloud?
>>We learn the sounds of the engines
>>>Heinkel, Junkers, Dormer, Messerschmitt

>>Clear day today though
>>>Too clear
>>>>Don't like it don't like it

LEN (*aside*). People sleeping rough everywhere. Washing hung on trees, empties in the grass. So many, I didn't realise fear's undone so many.

JACKIE sees FRED, sitting by the family's things. She is shocked.

JACKIE. Oh Len.

Dad!

A pause.

FRED. Jack.

Then they rush at each other. He drops the firewood. They embrace. They separate and are rowing.

JACKIE. What the bloody hell do you think you're doing, Dad?

FRED. Fighting the war my way, what do you think?

JACKIE. By dying up here of pneumonia?

FRED. At least it's a choice!

JACKIE. Where are Mum and Ma?

FRED. Out socialising. It's a new Little England up here. Under the greenwood tree.

LEN. That what you trying to do? Turn into Robin Hood?

FRED. Something like.

He coughs, heavily.

JACKIE. Oh, I could kick you, you silly, stubborn, lovely, stupid man – come home.

FRED. Government took my home.

LEN. Listen to me, Fred. It's chaos at Dimmock's with the machine tools. The electrics keep shorting, the coolant water floods the drains.

FRED. Got Supermarine knickers in a twist, has she, the old place?

LEN. We really need you, it's a bloody mess. Come back. Sort it out. I've talked to Beaverbrook. We'll make you the manager, train up your workers alongside Supermarine's. You'll run the place.

A pause.

FRED. No.

LEN. It's your patriotic duty.

FRED. I'm fighting for my country in my own way!

LEN. Jackie, knock some sense into him. If you don't, God help me, I'll put the police onto him.

LEN *pauses, then exits.*

JACKIE. You've got something in your head, haven't you. That you're not saying. C'mon, Dad, I know you.

LEN. I don't want my business to make Nazi planes.

JACKIE. But they want it to make Spitfires –

FRED. And it'll end up making Messerschmitts.

JACKIE. That what this is all about? You think we're going to lose the war?

FRED. Course we're going to lose the war.

JACKIE. Defeatist stuff, Father –

FRED. We are defeated. Everyone in the town knows it. Government propaganda just won't let us say so. I can feel it, in my chest, choking my breath, I can feel the tramp of their boots, coming up Main Street. It's like Winston said. We've got to take to the woods, to the hills, and fight 'em. Beaches, woods, hills.

JACKIE. Polly showed me what she does at Supermarine.

FRED. Yeah.

JACKIE. The drawings. Incredible work. (*A beat.*) Maybe we – just got to – go on as if we're going to win.

FRED. 'As if'? Even though we know we're not going to? Bloody stupid way of thinking about things.

JACKIE. But when I saw Polly's drawings –

She sees LIL *and* MA *entering.* LIL *is carrying firewood. They look ill. They stare at* JACKIE.

A drumming sound begins, low but getting louder.

Oh my God, Mum looks terrible – Dad –

FRED. We got to learn to live this, no other way –

LIL. Jackie, you staying up here with us now? I'll make tea, though it takes a while on the fire.

MA. Come to help? Having the time of our lives up here. I'm setting up a still the other side of the lake.

JACKIE. You're mad, you know that? The three of you!

The drumming sound is loud.

Dad, talk to me! Talk to me!

FRED. I can't! I can't think, I can't –

LIL. Above the trees! Look! Hundreds!

A heavy raid in the Battle of Britain begins.

CHORUS.
> Clear day
> Coming in
>
> Over the Isle of Wight
> Coming in
>
> Junkers 88s
> Estimate ninety
>
> Fighter cover
> 109s and 110s
>
> Coming in
> Biggest raid yet
>
> Post Office, Post Office, clear the wires
>
> Telexes whirr the numbers
> High Command
>
> Get our boys in the air
> Get our boys in the air
>
> Oh God, more
> Wave after wave

LIL. Do you – do you think they're bombing Dimmock's?

Lights up on CHORUS NO. 2.

CHORUS NO. 2.
> The great maps all in harmony
> Red for enemy
> Black for friendly
> Number to show height

CHORUS NO. 1.
> Wave after wave

JACKIE. Dad – they need planes. Polly can draw 'em but we can make 'em.

BEAVERBROOK. How many planes has Dowding in reserve?

1ST OFFICER. How many in reserve?

2ND OFFICER. All fighters in the air.

CHORUS NO. 2.
    No reserves!
           No reserves!
    All our boys in the air!

FRED. 'As if', you said, what did you mean? As if what – the end of all this, we'll go back across to France? Take Berlin?

JACKIE. Yeah, and Hitler's going to die in his bunker.

1ST OFFICER. Don't show it on your face

2ND OFFICER. Maximum danger, maximum panic

1ST OFFICER. Don't show it
           not a flicker

FRED. As if all the boys will come home. And what, after the war –

JACKIE. Holidays, beaches in Italy, skiing in the Alps – we'll go anywhere we want.

FRED. No borders.

JACKIE. No borders.

FRED. I've lost my way, haven't I.

CHORUS NO. 1.
    More coming in
        Junkers 88
           Fighter cover

FRED. I've lost my way.

LIL. What you two talking about?

MA. Fred Dimmock, if you're beginning to think what I think you're beginning to think, what about the still over the lake –

JACKIE. As if we'll all be the same, all be friends, all free –

FRED. As if we're going to win.

JACKIE. As if we're going to win.

FRED. Even though we're bloody not going to.

Lights down on the family. [*NB. quick change here for the actor from* FRED *to* DOWDING.]

The Battle of Britain effects come to a climax.

A silence.

Then the CHORUS *speaks dryly, i.e. not in choric mode.*

CHORUS NO. 1.
So-called Battle of Britain.

CHORUS NO. 2.
One hundred and twelve days of it.

CHORUS NO. 1.
RAF aircraft lost:

CHORUS NO. 2.
One thousand, seven hundred and forty-four.

CHORUS NO. 1.
German aircraft lost:

CHORUS NO. 2.
One thousand, nine hundred and seventy-seven.

CHORUS NO. 1.
Luftwaffe airmen killed and missing:

CHORUS NO. 2.
Two thousand, five hundred and eighty-five.

CHORUS NO. 1.
RAF fighter pilots killed:

CHORUS NO. 2.
Seven hundred and eighteen.

Full CHORUS. *Choral mode.*

CHORUS.
And it never stops

Day raids
            Night raids

All run ragged
                    Round the clock

Blitz
            Blitz
Planes
            Planes
Give us more planes

All run ragged

More planes!

            More planes!

Scene Nine

Ministry.

BEAVERBROOK *and* DOWDING.

BEAVERBROOK. I will go to Winston.

DOWDING. No no.

BEAVERBROOK. Well, all he did was call it 'The Battle of Britain'. You won it!

DOWDING. My face doesn't fit. Never did.

BEAVERBROOK. Face, what does that matter?

DOWDING. Everything. Look at you.

BEAVERBROOK. My face is ugly as sin.

DOWDING. Well, there you are.

BEAVERBROOK. Good God, Hugh, did you just make a joke?

DOWDING. Don't think so.

   BEAVERBROOK *is seething. He paces away then paces back.*

BEAVERBROOK. Air Chief Marshal! They must reinstate you.

DOWDING. No. I'm out of step. When it comes to tactics in air warfare, I'm a rapier man, use a thin blade, sudden, surgical strikes. Save lives that way. But no. My colleagues in Air Command want to flatten Germany. The sledgehammer, not the blade. There will be terrible consequences in the cities. Ah well. I'll grow my roses and look up at the vapour trails.

BEAVERBROOK. True heroes are unsung.

DOWDING. Perhaps. But what matter. Spot of lunch?

BEAVERBROOK. Sorry, Hugh, hell of a hurry, I have to motor down to Southampton –

DOWDING. Of course. How's the shadow-factory programme?

BEAVERBROOK. Bloody chaos. Only twenty-one of thirty-five converted. I demanded the first plane in three weeks. Going to be more like six. Wish I could shoot a few people.

DOWDING. Tricky, given we are meant to be defending democracy.

BEAVERBROOK. There's a lot of personal crap.

DOWDING. And you don't care.

BEAVERBROOK. Start caring and we lose. We're going to need more and more fighters. Night bombing is coming. The Germans call it 'Blitz'.

DOWDING. Yes.

They smile.

Exit DOWDING.

BEAVERBROOK *stays on the stage.*

Scene Ten

The grounds of Hursley House. BEAVERBROOK, *impatient.*

BEAVERBROOK. Where is the bloody woman?

POLLY *enters, cigarette and lighter ready. She sees him and immediately pulls back.*

POLLY. Oh.

BEAVERBROOK. Miss Polly Stride, as my life dictates. Have you see your aristo lady friend?

POLLY. Lady Coo– no.

BEAVERBROOK. Fag break?

POLLY. Yes.

BEAVERBROOK. Ten minutes maximum, you know.

POLLY. I know the rules.

BEAVERBROOK. Do you?

She lights a cigarette. He watches her.

I sent a car for you.

POLLY. I sent it back.

BEAVERBROOK. That was kind of rude.

POLLY. I put something for you in the car.

BEAVERBROOK. You did? What?

POLLY. A great big 'no'.

BEAVERBROOK *laughs.*

BEAVERBROOK. I've told Len Gooch to make you more senior.

POLLY. He'd have done that anyway. I don't need your help.

BEAVERBROOK. No?

POLLY. I like men. But I don't want one like you.

He laughs.

BEAVERBROOK. It would have been The Ritz!

Ignoring that, POLLY *exits. He kicks the ground in irritation.*

Enter LADY COOPER, *a distance away. She is carrying a hunting rifle.*

Mary!

She ignores him, Walking away. She readies the gun.

Lady Cooper!

She lowers the gun.

We were going to talk.

LADY COOPER. I'm walking my land. Do you understand the power of land, Max?

BEAVERBROOK. I think of the *Daily Express* like a country I own, I guess. I –

LADY COOPER. You see the land as part of you. Like your flesh and blood are grown into it.

BEAVERBROOK. Mary, I am so sorry.

LADY COOPER. No, you're not.

BEAVERBROOK. I tried to stop the order against you, but I had no choice.

LADY COOPER. I just took two girls into a room in my house.

BEAVERBROOK. One of them a civilian, and, goddammit, it's no longer a room in your house. It's a highly sensitive, top-secret area.

LADY COOPER. Which I just – waltzed into.

BEAVERBROOK. People are being disciplined.

She aims the gun at something for a moment then lowers it.

LADY COOPER. Sylvia was not an alien, as you well know.

BEAVERBROOK. She was deemed to be.

LADY COOPER. And now I am deemed a major security risk?

BEAVERBROOK. The nation must come first.

LADY COOPER. 'The nation'.

BEAVERBROOK. Can you bring yourself to understand?

LADY COOPER. Oh, we can bring ourselves to understand all kinds of things, can't we.

BEAVERBROOK. After the war, you'll –

LADY COOPER. No, I'll never come back to this house. It's dead to me now.

A beat.

Then BEAVERBROOK *sees something.*

BEAVERBROOK. A deer. It's looking straight at us.

She raises the gun and fires.

You hit it! My God.

LADY COOPER. Goodbye, Max.

She exits.

BEAVERBROOK *alone for a moment.*

BEAVERBROOK (*aside*). A terrible thing, necessity. It leaves a bitter taste. But, end of a long day, a bottle of Bolly and a good malt with Winston washes all that away. Then you start the day ready to wreck a few more lives. As needs must.

He smiles. A blackout.

Scene Eleven

Laundry.

WORKERS *cross the stage pulling a trolley with a shiny roll of metal on it.*

FRED *and* LEN.

FRED. It's not good enough!

LEN. I'm pushing.

FRED. Do more than push – thump, kick, scream.

LEN. You got to be realistic.

FRED. Realistic? Making a vital component of a modern killing machine out of steel that's not there? Where's 'realistic'?

LEN. There's a national shortage of steel at this grade, Port Talbot got bombed again last night.

FRED. We're all getting bombed, that's no excuse. I'm not starting the presses till I know I got a reliable supply.

LEN. You got to start today. I promised Beaverbrook.

FRED. Don't say the 'B' word! I am doing this, not you, not your boss. Get it in your head – if there's no more steel in seven days I'll have to shut the presses down. You know that can do damage, those machine tools are temperamental, like bloody racehorses. So! Get on to supply at Supermarine and tell 'em to get their fingers out.

LEN. Fred, what is it happened to you and me?

FRED. Oh! You mean why aren't we mates no more, why in't we chums, in it all together? I tell you, Len Gooch, there will be payback for the likes of you. It's people like this family are going to win this war, then God help you and your masters.

LEN. I had to – I had to – You are bloody unfair.

FRED. It's all bloody unfair. Now, for fuck's sake, get on the blower to Supermarine. And tell 'em to start the presses.

LEN *turns away.*

LEN *(aside).* All the things you're scared will happen to you in a war. Some terrible injury. Leg blown away, blindness.

But you don't expect to lose – the respect of the people you love. (*A beat.*) Well, that's how it has to be.

LEN *exits.*

Off, a low drumming sound begins – the presses…

Enter LIL.

LIL. Are we ready yet?

FRED. The presses are working.

LIL. The place smells so different. All oily.

FRED. Yeah. Funny, what's the smell of peace to us? Bleach.

Enters JACKIE *in a uniform.*

JACKIE. Well? I'm here for the big moment. Is it ready?

They stare at her.

LIL. What you wearing?

JACKIE. Oh this. I've joined the ATA.

FRED. The what?

JACKIE. The Air Transport Auxiliary. There's a training school at Hamble.

FRED. Training? To do what?

JACKIE. Fly Spitfires.

FRED. Women can't fly!

JACKIE. Why the hell not?

LIL. You're going to fight –

JACKIE. No, not fight, they'll not let us, more's the pity. The planes aren't armed. But I'll fly new ones direct from Eastleigh to their squadrons. Polly showed me drawings for the new Spitfire. So beautiful. And later, it hit me – we're going to make part of a Spitfire in our laundry, so I'll fly one!

LIL. It is a very smart uniform.

JACKIE. Natty, in't it.

FRED. I absolutely forbid you to do this!

JACKIE. Why?

FRED. What if a Messerschmitt spots you in an unarmed plane? What do you want to be? A harebrained heroine, shot down?

JACKIE. Actually I didn't think about it. I just did it.

POLLY (*off*). Can someone please give me a hand here?

JACKIE. Polly?

She exits quickly.

LIL. You won't stop her.

FRED. No.

LIL. Can't stop what's going to happen to us, either.

FRED. No. I'm having a bit of a try though.

LIL. You still think we're going to lose, don't you, love.

FRED. I tell you, Lil, we win this war, we're going to have Beaverbrook and Churchill and the Len Gooches and all this Government, out! And a whole new world.

LIL. Yeah, Ma says all the grannies are saying that.

FRED. There we are then.

They smile.

Enter MA.

MA. I heard the presses start. Great unveiling on us, is it?

FRED. Nearly, Ma!

MA. Did you have it out with Len Gooch about supplies?

FRED. I did, Ma. He blamed it on Port Talbot. I felt like I was trying to give the whole nation a bollocking.

MA. It's not the nation needs the bollocking.

JACKIE and POLLY *pull a trolley on, something on it is covered by a tarpaulin.*

FRED. What the hell is that?

POLLY. It's a present from Lady Cooper. She's in London now but she asked me to get it smuggled down to you, from the house.

POLLY *pulls the tarpaulin away, revealing a dead deer.*

LIL. My giddy aunt.

POLLY. She said it's been hung and gutted.

LIL. Very nice.

POLLY (*to* JACKIE). Dreamt of poaching a deer, didn't you. Well, here it is.

MA. Look at the meat on that.

LIL. Makes you think.

FRED. Yeah. Times of plenty.

For a moment they contemplate it.

LIL. Better send it to Eddy Rose's round the back, he can butcher it –

MA. No, I will. Can only dream of what I can sell a pound of venison for on the QT.

JACKIE. It's a gift, Ma, for the whole town.

MA. We will see about that.

Enter LEN. *He carries a cloth bag.*

FRED. Ready?

LEN. Ready.

For a moment, LEN *and* FRED *are close.* LEN *gives him something in his hand.*

Enter celebrating WORKERS, MEN *and* WOMEN, *in celebration mood, applauding.*

Ladies and gents, Dimmock family and friends. On behalf of Supermarine Company and the Ministry of Aircraft Production, I –

He stops. A pause. All embarrassed.

Fred, I think you should do this.

FRED. Well. It's ready. In just six weeks we've gone from washing long johns to aeronautical production. Funny to think we were a laundry, washing things… And what are we making for the mighty Spitfire?

He holds up a washer.

A washer.

All still. FRED *begins to laugh. Then they are all laughing.*

Not one washer, but lots 'n' lots o' washers. Planefuls and planefuls o' washers!

A siren sounds the alert.

Right. Volunteers to keep the machines going in the raid. Rest of you – Blitz drill.

For a second everyone is moving.

Blackout.

End Play.

A Nick Hern Book

The Shadow Factory first published in Great Britain as a paperback original in 2018 by Nick Hern Books Limited, The Glasshouse, 49a Goldhawk Road, London W12 8QP, in association with Nuffield Southampton Theatres

The Shadow Factory copyright © 2018 Howard Brenton

Howard Brenton has asserted his right to be identified as the author of this work

Cover image: Feast Creative

Designed and typeset by Nick Hern Books, London
Printed in the UK by Mimeo Ltd, Huntingdon, Cambridgeshire PE29 6XX

A CIP catalogue record for this book is available from the British Library

ISBN 978 1 84842 739 6